Rev. Dr. Neil Pembroke

Moving Toward
Spiritual Maturity
Psychological, Contemplative,
and Moral Challenges
in Christian Living

More pre-publication
REVIEWS, COMMENTARIES, EVALUATIONS . . .

"**I**n an era when spirituality is too readily overly psychologized, Pembroke offers a brilliant synthesis of the psychological, spiritual, and moral dimensions of Christian maturity. The description of this integrative journey to wholeness is fully consistent with the best of the Christian tradition. This book is essential reading for pastoral counselors, spiritually sensitive psychotherapists, spiritual directors, and ministry personnel."

Len Sperry, MD, PhD
Clinical Professor of Psychiatry,
Medical College of Wisconsin;
Author, *Transforming Self and Community:
Revisioning Pastoral Counseling
and Spiritual Direction*

The Haworth Pastoral Press®
An Imprint of The Haworth Press, Inc.
New York

Moving Toward Spiritual Maturity
Psychological, Contemplative, and Moral Challenges in Christian Living

THE HAWORTH PASTORAL PRESS®
Rev. James W. Ellor, DMin, DCSW, CGP
Melvin A. Kimble, PhD
Co-Editors in Chief

Moving Toward Spiritual Maturity
Psychological, Contemplative, and Moral Challenges in Christian Living

Rev. Dr. Neil Pembroke

The Haworth Pastoral Press®
An Imprint of The Haworth Press, Inc.
New York

For more information on this book or to order, visit
http://www.haworthpress.com/store/product.asp?sku=5886

or call 1-800-HAWORTH (800-429-6784) in the United States and Canada
or (607) 722-5857 outside the United States and Canada
or contact orders@HaworthPress.com

Published by

The Haworth Pastoral Press®, an imprint of The Haworth Press, Inc., 10 Alice Street, Binghamton, NY 13904-1580.

Library of Congress Cataloging-in-Publication Data

Pembroke, Neil.
    Moving toward spiritual maturity : psychological, contemplative, and moral challenges in Christian living / Neil Pembroke.
        p. cm.
    Includes bibliographical references and index.
    ISBN: 978-0-7890-3365-9 (hard : alk. paper)
    ISBN: 978-0-7890-3366-6 (soft : alk. paper)
    1. Spiritual formation. 2. Psychology, Religious. 3. Spiritual life—Christianity. 4. Christian ethics. I. Title.

BV4511.P44 2007
248.8'4—dc22
                                                                                            2006038044

For my wife, Janelle, my best friend
and always an inspiration.

ABOUT THE AUTHOR

Neil Pembroke, PhD, is senior lecturer in pastoral studies in the School of History, Philosophy, Religion, and Classics at the University of Queensland, Brisbane, Australia. Neil has a PhD in the area of pastoral care and counseling from New College, the University of Edinburgh. He is a member of the International Academy of Practical Theology. His other publications include *The Art of Listening: Dialogue, Shame, and Pastoral Care; Working Relationships: Spirituality in Human Service and Organisational Life;* and *Renewing Pastoral Practice: Trinitarian Perspectives on Pastoral Care and Counseling.*

CONTENTS

Introduction

Recently, my wife and I were watching a current affairs program on the television. The issue under discussion was the government initiative to provide a higher level of health care and other support services to elderly persons in order to help them stay longer in their own homes. In the segment that we were particularly engaged by, the reporter was interviewing a married couple in their late eighties. During the course of the interview, the husband indicated that they had lived in the same home for sixty years. He told the reporter how much they appreciated the support they were receiving; they were not ready to leave this home that has meant so much to them. As we watched, my wife made the comment that she could not imagine what it would be like to live for so long in the same house. Like so many in the baby-boomer generation, we have led a gypsy-like existence.

Though it has not been part of my personal experience, I can appreciate that there is something very nice about living in the same house for a very long period. It becomes the focal point for a host of experiences and memories that have shaped one's personal and familial life. Each new day, one renews contact with the home, and at the same time renews contact with those defining experiences.

If I were going to live in a home for sixty years, however, I, with my wife, would need to renovate it from time to time. The look of a house becomes dull and stale after a few years. It's important to maintain it as a fresh and vibrant living space.

This book is about renovation. Like the family home that one has lived in for so many years, one's spiritual life can become a bit too comfortable; it can lose its freshness and vitality. Therefore, it needs constant renewing. Now God's agent of spiritual renovation is the Spirit, and the Spirit blows where she wills. The task before us is therefore quite a bit subtler than that of home renovation. If I want to

Moving Toward Spiritual Maturity
© 2007 by The Haworth Press, Inc. All rights reserved.
doi:10.1300/5886_a

make over my home, I simply make the necessary arrangements (for either a do-it-yourself or a professional project) and it's done. The Holy Spirit, on the other hand, cannot be organized. The Spirit is free and her ways are mysterious. But we can organize *ourselves* so that we are ready and willing as the Spirit blows through us.

In this book, we will open three windows for God's transforming grace to blow through. These openings for divine action are *personal psychology, prayer and contemplation,* and the *moral life.*[1] Now persons are holistic entities and the lives we live cannot be neatly divided up into three categories. There is inevitably a good deal of cross-flow through the windows. It is not possible to talk about psychological development in a Christian person, for example, without introducing faith and moral questions. And the same can be said for the other two categories; there is a similar cross-ventilation that takes place. The benefit in dividing up our discussion of progress toward Christian maturity in this way is that it allows us to concentrate on the three quite different and vital perspectives each category brings. When we introduce the psychological, we are concerned with *mental, emotional,* and *interpersonal* dynamics. The spiritual sphere involves us in reflections about *prayer* and *the life of contemplation.* Last, in using the moral category we concentrate on *character* and on what is *right and good.*

In setting the scene for these explorations into certain central psychological, spiritual, and moral aspects of growth in the Christian life, consideration will be given to the place of personal fulfillment in the life of the Christian (Chapter 1). The suggestion here will be that self-fulfillment is something that happens while we are concentrating on being faithful to God's calling. We are called to cooperate with God in God's project of healing, reconciliation, and justice. Vocation rather than fulfillment is the primary concern for the disciple. The various discussions in this book, in one way or another, are about living one's vocation ever more faithfully.

In the first part of the book, where we will concentrate on psychological growth, the central theme is personal *wholeness*. We will see that our aim should be completeness, not perfection. In seeking to be faithful to the call to conformity to Christ, the perfect one, Christians often find themselves caught in the trap of perfectionism. It is important that we know how to break free of it.

We will begin by considering the task of reforming the wayward parts or "subselves" in our personhood. There is within each one of us a center of identity and initiative that shapes our way of being in the world. We call this the self. But psychologists tell us that sitting under the governance of this unitary self is a community of subselves. In a particular individual, then, one might find a loving self, an aggressive self, a fearful self, a creative self, a parent self, a prayerful self, a controlling self, and a clumsy self, to name just a few of the possibilities. I will be suggesting that what is vitally important is that we get to know this community well, and in particular, that we act to reform wayward selves. If we have subselves that cause damage to self and others—what I will refer to as "morally relevant" selves— we need to work on mitigating their destructive tendencies.

In taking up the challenge of reforming wayward subselves, however, there is always a danger that we will fall into moral perfectionism. Christians are especially vulnerable to this emotional and spiritual scourge. Mindful of the words of Jesus, "You are to be perfect, as your heavenly Father is perfect," we find ourselves compulsively pursuing impossibly high ideals. Faced with our inevitable failures, we are overcome by feelings of failure and guilt. In looking for a way forward, we will take up the view of the eminent Swiss psychotherapist, Carl Jung, that a person should aim for wholeness or completeness rather than perfection. In Jung's thinking, we are moving toward wholeness when we attempt to reconcile our inner opposites. A theological perspective will complement this psychological approach. From the point of view of faith, we are made whole by Christ's saving grace.

Along with moral or guilt-based perfectionism, there is achievement or shame-based perfectionism. We can fall into the trap of driving ourselves to higher and higher levels of achievement in life in the vain hope of transcending feelings of shame. Feeling inadequate and flawed, we aim to establish our self-worth through the outcomes of our efforts in the school or university, in the workplace, or on the sporting field. I will point out that the core belief that is operational here is "I am what I achieve." The notion of core beliefs comes from cognitive therapy. In this therapeutic approach, the aim is to reshape distorted patterns of thinking. Using the belief modification approaches developed by the cognitive therapists, I will attempt to show how a tendency to shame-based perfectionism can be countered.

In the second part of the book, our reflections on prayer and contemplation will be organized around the notion of *conversion*. For some, conversion means a defined moment or period in a person's life when a conscious decision was made to turn to Christ. This is indeed a conversion. There is also, however, the ongoing work of conforming one's life more closely to Christ, and this too is a conversion. The task for us is to attend to God's voice in our daily lives as God calls us to greater conformity to Christ. The theme of the everyday will be an important one. We do not find God only in quiet places of prayer. We can also tune into God in the hustle and bustle of daily life. If we are to hear the Spirit calling through the common experiences of our lives, we need the discipline of prayer. I will develop a notion of "storied prayer." A story begins sometime back then ("Once upon a time . . ."); brings the plot alive so that it feels as if it is happening right now; and leads us into the future ("And they all lived happily [or not so happily] ever after . . ."). Storied prayer has a past, a present, and a future tense. It is a way of praying that invites God to take us through all the temporal dimensions of our existence as we seek to move forward with God.

An important dimension in conversion to Christ is the moral one. The theme running through the final part of the book is *responsibility.* To act in a responsible manner means to be accountable for our decisions and actions, and to be responsive to the claims of others. Responsibility and conscience are closely connected. Critical introspection reveals our failures in responsible living. In Chapter 8, conscience will be linked to moral vision. We have a vision of the way interpersonal, societal, and international relationships should be ordered. That vision is shaped by the central Christian values of compassion, justice, and peace. From time to time, however, we encounter situations that run counter to this vision. We find ourselves caught up in what some call "contrast experiences." These are experiences that contrast with our moral vision of the way human life should be ordered. Faced with the contrast, our conscience will direct us to take some action to improve the situation. We will reflect on how contrast experiences challenge us and, through the responses we make, give a particular shape to our lives.

Love is clearly central in a responsible life. We will take up this theme in Chapter 9. Giving of oneself for the sake of others is agape. The love ideal that has been commonly put before the Christian community is one of self-sacrifice. Christ sacrificed himself for the world, we are told, and therefore we too should be prepared to offer ourselves for others. With this in mind, many Christians feel pangs of guilt whenever they pay attention to their own needs and desires. The love ethic that I will describe frees people from this spiritual bind. It posits equality between self-love and other-love. To be responsible, a Christian must love others neither more nor less than oneself.

Last, three virtues that are at the heart of the responsible life will be discussed. These are integrity, courage, and compassion. A virtue is really a habit—or at least that is the way the great medieval theologian, Thomas Aquinas, thought of it. If I have the virtue of courage, for example, I will be ready to act courageously when the situation demands it. In the final chapter, I will attempt to show how these three "habits" enable us to live responsibly in the world.

This, then, is the plan for our spiritual renovations. In order to get us ready for the main task, we will look at the fundamental issue of the relationship between personal fulfillment and the Christian vocation.

PART I:
SETTING THE SCENE

Chapter 1

Self-Fulfillment and Vocation

This is a book about growing into spiritual maturity. The first "window" that we will open in our search for wisdom and insight is psychotherapeutic psychology. In our therapeutic culture, self-fulfillment is something that is valued very highly. We desperately want to live lives of meaning and purpose—lives that are permeated with happiness and a sense of well-being. In a word, we aspire to full humanness. In fact, this is Abraham Maslow's word. The term *self-actualization* is more frequently associated with Maslow, but full humanness was for him a more descriptive term.[1] In order to progress toward the goal of being fully human, a person needs to know herself and her potential and to actively reach out for it.

Maslow (along with others in the humanist stream of psychology) believes that it is through realizing our physical, emotional, intellectual, and spiritual[2] potential that we experience personal fulfillment. These psychological theorists have much to teach us about the journey to psychospiritual maturity. From a Christian perspective, however, their approach suffers from a serious flaw. It is founded on an assumption of self-groundedness (perhaps the most serious of the modern heresies, according to James Fowler[3]). The primary concern for those of us who are disciples of Christ, I will be suggesting, should not be with self-fulfillment, but rather with living our vocation. God calls us to incarnate God's love in the world. It is as we live faithful to this calling that we experience fulfillment. Fulfillment is something that happens while one is living in and through love for God and for neighbor.

Moving Toward Spiritual Maturity
© 2007 by The Haworth Press, Inc. All rights reserved.
doi:10.1300/5886_01

PSYCHOLOGICAL APPROACHES
TO PERSONAL FULFILLMENT

Martin is a talented accountant. He's always been a very organized and careful person. The order, logic, and precision associated with accountancy fits his personality extremely well. He's very good at what he does. Martin is rewarded handsomely for his contribution to the firm, and his colleagues are good to work with. Ask Martin about his work and he'll tell you that he loves it.

Sadly, Martin is not as happy as one might think. The inner turmoil that he has to contend with has nothing to do with his personal life. He is married to a lovely woman, Janette, and they share their life with three fine children. Martin is not worried, either, about his physical appearance. He is a fine specimen of manhood. Martin is not bored, and nor is he stressed. The absence of the spiritual dimension is not the issue. He is not a regular churchgoer, but he finds real peace and strength through prayer and meditation.

So what *is* the problem? Martin's unhappiness stems from the fact that he is plagued by a lack of self-confidence. This adversely affects the way he works. Its impact is especially strong when he meets a new client. Though he knows that he is a good accountant, he finds himself trying too hard to prove that to the client. Martin would love to be able to relax and simply trust in his ability.

Martin's lack of self-confidence also caused him to pull back from a very important opportunity that came his way. Last month, he was offered a partnership in his firm. Janette and he talked long and hard about the offer. While she was convinced that taking it was right for him, Martin was not so sure. He felt that he was not ready for it at this stage. "Give me another few years," he told her, "and I'll have the experience I need." In his honest moments alone, he realized that he was hiding from the truth. He was more than ready. The reason he chose to turn the offer down was that he was scared. He was afraid of failing, and he was afraid of succeeding.

Martin has settled for a "regression choice" (Maslow). Unless he can find the inner strength to make some crucial changes, he will never realize his full potential. In order to move toward full humanness, a person must become increasingly self-aware. "A very important part of this task," writes Maslow, "is to become aware of what one *is,* biologically, temperamentally, constitutionally, as a member of a species, of one's capacities, desires, needs, and also of one's vocation, what one is fitted for, what one's destiny is."[4] Finding one's mission in life, then, involves "opening oneself up to himself."[5]

Reaching out for our destiny requires a willingness to make the choices that will carry us forward. The decisions we make in life, says Maslow, fall into two camps.[6] On the one hand, there are "progression" or "growth" choices, and on the other, "regression" or "fear" choices. Those on the way to full humanness are not afraid to choose paths that challenge and stretch them. They are aware that the growth choice carries with it a significant risk of failure, but they are prepared to take on that risk for the sake of progression toward self-actualization.

It is a matter of learning to face the challenges life presents with honesty, truthfulness, and courage. "A person who does each of these . . . things each time the choice point comes," reflects Maslow,

> will find that they add up to better choices about what is constitutionally right for him. He comes to know what his destiny is . . . what his mission in life will be. One cannot choose wisely for a life unless he dares to listen to himself, *his own self,* at each moment in life.[7]

Rollo May refers to this process of embracing the truth of one's life as *choosing oneself* (using a term coined by the father of existentialism, Søren Kierkegaard). When I choose the self that is genuinely me, I am truly free. Indeed, freedom—a favorite theme of the existentialists—is the key concept in May's analysis.

Freedom refers to a person's "capacity to take a hand in [her] own development."[8] If a person is to do this, she must be self-aware. Without consciousness of the self, she is at the mercy of her own unconscious drives as well as a whole range of external forces. In the absence of self-awareness, there is no possibility of taking control of the unfolding of one's life. One is simply pushed and pulled through life. "That consciousness of self and freedom go together," writes May,

> is shown in the fact that the less self-awareness a person has, the more [she] is unfree. That is to say, the more [she] is controlled

by inhibitions, repressions, childhood conditionings which [she] has consciously "forgotten" but which still drive [her] unconsciously, the more [she] is pushed by forces over which [she] has no control.[9]

Dorothy Rowe also makes this connection between creating personal meaning and freedom. Too often we forfeit our freedom as human beings, observes Rowe, because our nerve fails us. We fall away from our responsibility for creating our own truths, our own way of being. Instead, we regress to the blissful state in which powerful others (e.g., Mom and Dad) shaped our world for us. Thus, we hand over our responsibility to the state, the church, and the international cartels.[10] To take responsibility for the construction of our own universes of meaning is scary, and hence we hand over our freedom to others. We may feel less anxious, but the cost is too high. When we fail to take responsibility for ourselves, we lose the joy of being. To find joy, meaning, and fulfillment in life, we need to live our freedom. This freedom is not "willful selfishness," however.

> This "freedom" is no freedom at all, for the person indulging in such "freedom," be he a soccer hooligan or a dishonest industrialist, is not free but is driven by an insatiable hunger for he knows not what. The freedom of which I speak is the freedom to recognize and to use our capacity to choose. In such freedom we experience ourselves as neither driven by outside forces and demands, nor imprisoned and inhibited by outside barriers and our own fear, guilt and shame. Freely making our own choices, we stand behind what we choose. Freely we choose to accept responsibility for ourselves. Freely we choose to make commitments. Free, we do not fear freedom.[11]

Any discussion of freedom must pay attention to the role of determinism. There is a whole range of factors beyond a person's control that will have a very significant impact on the final form of her life. The culture of her country of birth, the values and attitudes in her family of origin, the gifts/abilities and the traits/tendencies associated with her genetic inheritance, together with a number of other factors, are determinative to a very significant extent of her destiny.

May argues, though—following the existentialists—that there is one freedom that determinism can never remove, and that is the freedom to *choose* the facts of one's life. That is, one can freely accept the realities rather than treat them as imposed. A person who would love to be a great artist can find peace and fulfillment in accepting the fact that she lacks the talent to reach that far. She can't choose to be a great painter, but she can choose to love her art and the creations that come from her hand, even though part of her would like them to be so much better. On a higher, more dramatic level, Socrates chose his cup of hemlock over compromise, and Jesus chose his cup of suffering over infidelity. "Thus," reflects May, "freedom is not just the matter of saying 'Yes' or 'No' to a specific decision: it is the power to mold and create ourselves. Freedom is the capacity, to use Nietzsche's phrase, 'to become what we truly are.'"[12]

In order to be free, to take responsibility for shaping one's life, courage is required. As we have already seen, it is easier to let others decide for you. It takes inner fortitude to choose one's own path. A person needs the courage to listen to her "impulse voices" rather than to introjected parental voices.[13] What is required is "the willingness to differentiate, to move from the protecting realms of parental dependence to new levels of freedom and integration."[14] This assertion of autonomy, this break from external control and direction, is a challenge that is not only a factor at critical times such as beginning school and the adolescent identity crisis, but right through a person's life. It involves being prepared to step outside of the boundaries that others have constructed in defining acceptable or normal attitudes and behaviors. There is security in following the patterns of values, thinking, and action that the family, the church, and the society establish in consensus. To follow an inner direction that challenges the normative patterns creates fear and uncertainty. "Courage," writes May, "is the capacity to meet the anxiety which arises as one achieves freedom."[15] This is not to say that freedom is just another name for rebellion. A compulsive need to rebel constitutes another form of bondage. To *have* to be different is not the same as *choosing* one's own path; indeed, it speaks more of insecurity than of liberation. To pass over the difficult task of evaluating consensus values and attitudes and move to a quick and easy dismissal of their worth is to fall away from freedom and into license. "Rebellion acts as a substitute for the more difficult process of struggling through to one's own autonomy, to new beliefs, to the state where one can lay new foundations on which to build."[16]

Courage is also indissolubly linked to truth. One is reminded of Jesus' words "And you shall know the truth, and the truth shall set you free" (Jn 8:32). Knowing the truth is not so much a function of intelligence, of learning, and of a store of facts, but rather of finding the courage to see what is really in oneself, in one's family, and in the world around one. Ultimately the courage that is called for is the courage to cast off our defenses and neurotic needs. Our repressions, conflicts, and defense mechanisms cause us to distort inner and outer reality. They lead us to project our prejudices, failings, fears, and expectations onto others and the world around us. The way of courage-seeking-truth, then, is the way of self-awareness. "[I]t is precisely the lack of self-awareness," observes May,

> which leads us to call error truth. The more a person lacks self-awareness, the more [she] is prey to anxiety and irrational anger and resentment: and while anger generally blocks us from using our more subtle intuitive means of sensing truth, anxiety always blocks us.[17]

Personal fulfillment, observes Dorothy Rowe, is not about having everything, but rather about realizing that the best is good enough. To live in and through self-awareness, truth, courage, and creativity is to be truly free—that is the best that life has to offer. Toward the end of her book, however, Rowe points out that from her list of what is best in life she has omitted love.[18] She takes some time to get to this central human concern and experience because it is so often misunderstood. In the place of confused and sentimentalized versions of love she suggests that we interpret it as "gentle, strong, boundless, secure, fearless, joy, contentment, bliss of being."[19]

The enemies of this "true love" are fear and hate. Where there is fear there is a barrier that keeps love out. And of course, love cannot exist where there is hatred. Hate can be strong and total, as in hatred for one's enemies. Or it can be milder and more specific, as in the hatred one might have for certain aspects of the beloved. True love transcends these blocks through approaching the other as an equal. With all our flaws and inferiorities, as well as all our gifts and strengths, we struggle together in the face of life's uncertainties and peculiarities. Neither you nor I can assert superiority in this struggle, for we are both simply doing our best. Here is the basis for mutuality in relationship, and through such mutuality true love is expressed.

It is noteworthy that nowhere in her discussion of love does Rowe uphold the value of self-giving. To the contrary, she champions "an enlightened self-interest" and suggests that self-sacrifice is "a waste."[20] Now of course self-sacrifice and self-giving cannot simply be equated. The latter term makes room for appropriate self-regard, whereas the former tends to imply its absence. But it is clear enough that giving-of-self-for-the-other has only a relatively small place in Rowe's conception of love. She can happily talk about it in terms of security, contentment, fearlessness, joy (bliss even), and equality, but she does not see a need to commit herself to the ideal of self-giving.

Rollo May and Abraham Maslow, on the other hand, are quite a bit stronger on the importance of making oneself available for others. May has written extensively about human love. He shows how the three loves—*eros, philia,* and *agape*—are interrelated.[21] Eros is desire, the experience of being pulled toward the other. Philia is friendship love. It is established through the mutuality and reciprocity shared by friends. May points out that eros needs philia. The sexual tension needs to be dissipated; the lovers need to be able to simply relax in each other's presence. Particularly relevant to our discussion is May's observation that philia, in turn, needs agape. Genuine friendship is built on disinterested love. Agape is grounded in a concern for the other's well-being that is (largely) free of calculations of personal gain (May rightly points out that human love is never totally disinterested).

Maslow, for his part, lists amongst his "B-Values" (the values of being)[22] goodness and justice. The self-actualizing person actively promotes what is right and good. That is, she recognizes the importance of "living outside [her] skin."

We have already begun the process of reflecting on the question of the fit between self-actualization theory and Christian teaching. It is time to pursue it more fully.

CONTINUITIES AND DISCONTINUITIES
WITH THE CHRISTIAN TRADITION

First, the idea that self-awareness is essential if a person is to grow and develop is congruent with a theological anthropology. A fundamental goal for disciples is the conforming of the self ever more fully to the way of Christ. We are to have our minds and our spirits renewed (Rom 12:1-2) as we engage with life. Through the internal and external challenges in life we have an opportunity to develop our mental, emotional, moral, and spiritual potentialities. But in order to make the most of this opportunity, we need to be aware of, and to be dealing with, the blocks in our lives. If there are significant defenses and neurotic tendencies that we never acknowledge and therefore never seek to transcend, this will be impossible. The strong emphasis the psychological theorists give to self-awareness is very appropriate from a Christian perspective.

Second, the notion that selfishness holds a person back from full humanness fits with the Christian ethical system. May recognizes the importance of making oneself available for the other. Agape is for him a virtue that all persons who value psychological and spiritual health will seek to cultivate. Maslow, too, advocates concern for the well-being of others. A person who chases after self-actualization as a trophy to be won is missing the point totally. She needs to be converted to a way of life that includes promoting truth, goodness, and justice. Similarly, Rowe points out that freedom cannot be found in "willful selfishness." Now she does promote the idea of "enlightened self-interest," and consequently it may be thought that selfishness is allowed into her thinking in a disguised form. Although there is some truth in this, it needs to be borne in mind that the "enlightened" aspect of the term indicates an awareness of the fact that love cannot be sustained unless there is give as well as take in a relationship. Of course, this is quite a way from the Christian conception of agape. The point that I am making is simply that Maslow, May, and Rowe all argue that selfishness constitutes a block on the journey to full humanness. Moreover, this is congruent with gospel values.

Maslow's idea of growth versus fear choices is also an important one. It is evident that we are all confronted with a number of challenges in life. Where there is a challenge, the fear of failure looms large. If we consistently fall away when the testing times come along, there is no possibility of growth. The story of the saints of the church is one of being unafraid to follow the Spirit's lead along difficult and uncharted paths.

Indeed, as all our psychological theorists point out, human existence requires that we walk a difficult road. We are caught up in a life-long journey of choosing the self. This is our freedom. To be sure, a Christian chooses a way-of-being-in-the-world in dialogue with God. She is constantly seeking divine guidance and wisdom. But even with the knowledge that the Spirit Friend is walking every step with her, fear does not disappear and courage does not become redundant. The psychologists are right to point out that without the virtues of honesty and inner fortitude diminution of the self is inevitable.

There are clearly a number of positives, then, in the three psychological approaches to personal fulfillment. In seeking to grow and develop as persons, there is much that we can learn from Maslow, May, and Rowe. Indeed, it is fair to say that in them we find genuine wisdom to guide us on life's journey. In a theological perspective, however, there is a serious flaw that they are all affected by. Here James Fowler's observations are particularly enlightening. In reviewing theories of self-actualization and personal fulfillment quite similar to the ones that we have looked at, he suggests that they represent "what may be our most serious modern heresy, the individualistic assumption that we are or can be *self-grounded persons*."[23] This assumption means that we have within us all the resources that are necessary to find fulfillment and to actualize our full humanity. Above self-actualization, Fowler places *vocation*. Growing into maturity, in a Christian perspective, involves embracing God's calling into partnership with all the faith, energy, commitment, and love that one can muster. The call of God is to join in partnership in God's project for the world. It is a project that aims at the promotion of peace, justice, righteousness, and reconciliation. In essence, it involves giving oneself in love for people and for the natural world.

More recently, theologian Gary Badcock has presented a very similar view. The vocation of the Christian, he says, is to a love that expresses itself through cross-bearing. Thus, "[i]t is not *primarily* about self-discovery or self-fulfillment . . . but about finding one's life by losing it for Christ's sake."[24] Although our primary concern should not be with personal fulfillment, there is certainly a place for it in the life of discipleship. "[T]here is absolutely nothing unchristian," writes Badcock, "about seeking true fulfillment in the service of God: to quote Jesus, 'those who lose their life for my sake will find it' (Mt 16:25)."

Self-fulfillment is not selfish when it is set in the context of vocation. Indeed, it can be seen as "the actualization of the 'human potential' for worship, obedience, and service."[25] Christians join with those outside of faith in desiring a sense of fulfillment in life, but our focus is different. In cooperating with the Spirit in developing our personal potential, a central aim is to provide God with a richer array of resources for use in the divine project in the world. If our primary commitment is to serve God, personal development is seen not only simply as a good in and of itself, but also as a resource that we can offer to God and to others.

Personal fulfillment comes out of focusing on living out one's vocation of love in the world. To establish full realization of the self as one's first and last goal in life is not appropriate. The primary goal for those of us who are disciples, rather, is to convert ourselves to the way of agape and so to share in God's work of building joy, peace, justice, and reconciliation in the world. It is as we engage ourselves fully in straining after this goal that we begin to experience fulfillment. Personal fulfillment should not be our *chief* concern, but it will naturally be on our list. We need not worry about whether or not it will come, however. In living out our vocation of love we find our meaning and our purpose; that is, we find ourselves. How could it be otherwise, for to live in love is to live in God. When we experience the love and grace of God, we are in touch with the deepest meaning of our existence.

But what does it mean, exactly, to live the vocation of love? Badcock offers us a helpful lead with his notion of cross-bearing. However, one wishes that he would have paid attention to the relationship between self-giving and self-love. His ideas will be outlined, and then some comments will be made about what is deficient in his approach.

THE WAY OF LOVE

The way of love, observes Badcock, is the way of the cross-bearing.[26] In today's world we do not usually think of this, as the earliest Christians would have, in terms of martyrdom. Rather, we think of something more modest: to carry one's cross is to engage in acts of service. But as Badcock points out, the kind of service Christ asks us to engage in is anything but modest. We would have to find another description altogether to cover actions such as loving enemies, praying for persecutors, and lighting up the way to God. Indeed, we would refer to such actions with descriptors such as "hard," "challenging," and, perhaps the most apt of all, "costly."

Badcock enlists Martin Luther and the Swiss-German Catholic theologian Hans Urs von Balthasar to shape his reflections on the costly service we are called to. Luther sees Christian service as fundamentally love for neighbor. In this way, we have an opportunity to address the sin within. For at base, sin is a form of selfishness. In turning to the other in love, we die to self and therefore to sin.

There is, however, Badcock points out, a shortcoming in Luther's approach. This shortcoming is present in all of his theology and has to do with the two kingdoms doctrine. According to Luther, the vocation of love belongs to the kingdom of law, but not to the kingdom of heaven. Our loving actions on behalf of our neighbor are of no use in heaven. But if our good works, observes Badcock, are of no avail as far as the kingdom of heaven is concerned, why does God command them?

It is at this point that Badcock finds Balthasar's doctrine of vocation helpful. The Swiss theologian contends that the whole purpose in the saving action of God in Christ's life, death, and resurrection is personalizing and humanizing human beings. Disciples are called to share in the ongoing mission of Christ; that is, to bear his cross. In order to live in the way of suffering love in the world, we must enter into the mind of Christ. To live in and through a mind conformed to Christ is to take up his attitude of selflessness and his willingness to sacrifice himself for others. All around us, in the little things and in the big things of life, we find opportunities to give of ourselves for the sake of others. As Badcock puts it: "One does not . . . have to look far to find a cross to bear . . . It is . . . the cross of self-giving, of bearing the sins of others for the sake of reconciliation, and thus the cross of love that must often entail suffering."[27]

BALANCING SELF-GIVING AND SELF-LOVE

While it is clear that Christ calls us to self-giving in seeking the fulfillment of others, he also recognizes the importance of love of self: "You shall love your neighbour as yourself" (Mt 22:39). I am concerned about the fact that in talking about our Christian vocation Badcock stresses the importance of the self-giving—and even of the self-sacrifice—that constitutes cross-bearing, without also stressing the need for self-love. It is not that he is unaware of the need for love of self. He says in one place: "In order to love another, one must be able also to love oneself."[28] But this passing reference is all that we find. The balancing of self-giving and self-loving is a vitally important concern and it demands a full treatment. To achieve this balance is no easy task; it requires a highly nuanced discussion. Such a discussion will have to wait until Chapter 9.

If those of us who are engaged in service and advocacy are not sufficiently kind to ourselves, we quite rapidly experience the demands of discipleship overwhelming us. Everywhere we look there is a need; suffering, violence, and injustice are all around us. We need to find a balance in our lives. There needs to be a (rough) equality in the relationship between self-love and self-giving. We are called to love others neither more nor less than we love ourselves. Sometimes the term *equal regard* is used to describe this principle. In fact, because the pull of selfishness can be quite strong, we probably need to put a "practical swerve" (G. Outka) to the neighbor in place. That is, we need to push ourselves to consider fully the needs of the other person lest we unwittingly tip the balance in favor of our own needs. We may be thinking that the principle of equal regard is guiding us, but in fact selfishness has slipped in without our awareness. A practical swerve needs to be put in place to make sure there really is a balance between self-love and other-love. Clearly, this is a reasonably complex issue, and much more will be said later. The point I am trying to make here is simply that it is unhelpful to advocate cross-bearing without at the same time showing how this can be balanced with taking care of our own legitimate needs and aspirations.

Let me try to draw the key ideas in our discussion together. Christians have every right to be concerned about personal fulfillment, but we should not make it our primary concern. We need to seek first the reign of God's love and justice in the world. Self-fulfillment comes as a by-product of cooperating with God in God's project. Engaging faithfully with the challenges of life in God's Realm is our primary vocation in life. This whole book, let me say, is about what it means to live faithful to this calling.

Actualizing human potential flows from wholehearted, *reflective* participation in God's project in the world. I have emphasized the word "reflective" because I want to indicate that self-actualization is not an automatic process for the disciple of Christ. The psychological theorists we have studied point to an important reality that we ignore at our peril. Our primary focus, I have said, needs to be on worship, service, and the cause of justice and peace. Living faithful to our calling provides all the scope we need for self-realization. But it does not follow that developing greater self-awareness as advocated by the therapists is simply an optional extra. While we may be dedicated Christians making a significant contribution, we may still be trapped in our own pain and dysfunctionality and, consequently, hurt others through our personal deficiencies. The reason for this is that we are insufficiently aware of the neurotic needs, defenses, and thought patterns that are pushing and pulling us around. We may be zealous in our acts of service and advocacy, but we are quite a way from psycho-spiritual wholeness. It is to a consideration of the vitally important issue of how we move toward such wholeness that we now turn.

PAI
TOWARD PSY
WHOL

Chapter 2

Wholeness in the Community of the Self

How do you think about the self, about the self that you are? We are all aware that there is a center of initiative within us that drives our thinking, willing, feeling, and acting. It is quite difficult, however, to conceptualize it. The self is an exceedingly subtle and elusive force in the psychology of the human person. Most, if not all, of us think of it as a (relatively) unified entity. We see the self as *a* center of initiative rather than as *centers* of initiative. But we are also aware that there is multiplicity—pluralism—in the life of the self. We often hear people make a comment along the lines, "I've got an aggressive side that comes out sometimes" or "I'm quite a shy person in one-to-one interactions, but strangely enough I'm quite comfortable speaking in front of a crowd." Or, to give one last example, a person may say, "I'm usually not particular fussy, but when it comes to my piano playing, I just have to get it just right."

Psychologists have noticed this interplay between unity and multiplicity in the life of the self. The way they formulate the relationship varies, but most refer to a superordinate self (a Self) that coordinates a cluster of subselves. On this view, then, there is within each of us a community of selves. The community is made up of—to give some common examples—a loving self, an aggressive self, an anxious self, a competitive self, a parental self, a romantic self, an intellectual self, a responsible self, and a fun-loving self. Now in order for this community to be "healthy," it is necessary to achieve a reasonably high level of understanding, acceptance, and harmony.

Moving Toward Spiritual Maturity
© 2007 by The Haworth Press, Inc. All rights reserved.
doi:10.1300/5886_02

All of us, to a greater or lesser extent, experience trouble in the community. To be sure, there are those selves that we like and that contribute to our sense of self-worth. But there are others that we are not so sure about. Indeed, some of them we dislike quite intensely. I want to approach the problem of strife in the community from two angles, namely *suppression* and *disowning*. There are subselves, first, which we would like to give full expression to but feel pressured into holding down. There are voices within, alien ones, which tell us that these selves are not acceptable in some way. Thus, we feel compelled to suppress them.

Disowning involves going a step further. This is so because our feelings toward a particular self are so strongly negative. A self that we are suppressing we may actually like. Some other voice is speaking against that self. Or it may be that a self is held down because we feel some discomfort when it is allowed expression (e.g., an angry self or an unconventional self). But there are also selves that we strongly dislike. These are representative of our weaknesses and inferiorities. The presence of these inferiorities causes us significant distress and we respond by rejecting them. If the level of discomfort is sufficiently high we may cut them off completely. That is, we no longer recognize them as belonging to the Self.

In order to achieve a higher degree of integration within the Self we need to deal with suppression and disowning. The first step is always recognizing and acknowledging the self that we have lost contact with. But the strategies from that point on are different. A suppressed self needs to be freed up, allowed to express itself. In this task we will benefit greatly from the intervention of a spiritual guide or trusted friend. We need others who will advocate for the self that is being held down.

A disowned self, on the other hand, needs to be embraced with love and acceptance. There are a number of therapeutic strategies available that are intended to facilitate this process. Often associated with these strategies, however, is a policy of declaring every self as "okay," as valid and acceptable. But I believe we need to ask the question: Is it appropriate to proclaim each and every part of the Self as "okay"? Here we see the tendency in some, probably most, secular counselors and therapists to turn a blind eye to the moral dimension of the Self.[1] Although there are some selves that are morally neutral and can be embraced just as they are, there are also those related to moral failure which, while they certainly need our love and acceptance, also need reformation.

In order to set the scene for our reflections, I will outline some attempts to describe how subselves function within the life of the Self. Although there are those who want to talk about a paradigm shift in the theory of selfhood, I believe that we can in fact find "communitarian thinking" in the older psychologies of Sigmund Freud, Carl Jung, Eric Berne, and Heinz Kohut. Moreover, these psychologies are particularly helpful in the attempt to understand the dynamics associated with suppression and disowning of selves. So we'll begin with insights associated with the new models, but we will also draw on those in the classic theories.

THE SELF AND ITS SUBSELVES

The British psychotherapist John Rowan has perhaps done the most to build our understanding of the communitarian nature of the Self. He was led to think about subselves—he uses the term "subpersonalities"—through his personal experience.[2] Through Gestalt therapeutic work he found himself discovering various "aspects" of his personality. Later, he began to realize that these aspects could be grouped together to form subpersonalities. He defines a subpersonality as "a semi-permanent and semi-autonomous region of the personality capable of acting as a person."[3]

He finds that in working with clients it is useful to give names to the various subpersonalities. Naming makes for easy reference, and more significantly, it makes the subpersonalities "more human and more approachable."[4] One of the examples Rowan offers refers to a thirty-five-year-old woman:

Carmen Miranda: Black, beautiful, dramatic, sensual, bitchy.

Earthy Mangold: Has children, animals, grows things, intuitive, compassionate. Can also be gossipy, dirty, lazy, sluttish.

Good Son: Very brave, never cries, tough, male.

Little Wilhelmina: Very suppressed, needs taking care of, doesn't like imposing on people. Needs to ask for love.

Apple Juice: Ascetic, meditates, wrapped up in mysticism, vegetarian. Wants to be balanced.

Mostly Me: Strong, independent, rather impatient, easily hurt, expects rejection and criticism. Can also be stiff-necked, proud, not to be comforted.[5]

Rowan observes that there are certain regularities in relation to subpersonalities.[6] There are selves that are common to a large number of people. For example, it is extremely common for persons to have at least one very unpleasant self. This self causes fear and distress and is difficult to deal with. But there is also usually at least one other subpersonality that is unafraid and able to handle it. Of course, while there are commonalities we also have our idiosyncratic selves.

It is interesting to note that another British psychotherapist, J. M. M. Mair, picked up the idea of subselves quite early.[7] Like Rowan, he advocates naming selves. He begins his discussion with a reference to the smallest form of community, namely a community of two persons. It is common to refer to being "in two minds." There is part of a person tending in a certain direction, but another part is pulling in the opposite direction. It is like having to battle with oneself. The community of two can be expanded to three, four, or more selves, Mair observes. Some of these selves will persist over time; others will play a role for only a limited time. Subselves may be "loners," or they may be "team players." Some will be powerful and dominant; others will be docile and agreeable.

Mair encourages his clients to reflect on their psychic conflicts in terms of their internal selves. He suggests that they may find it helpful to work with the "characters" provided by communities they are familiar with. These will be political groups, business communities, sporting clubs, and the like. So, for example, a client may choose politics as his context for working with his community of selves. He may decide to interpret himself in terms of "the Leader of the Opposition," "the Treasurer," and "the Lobbyist." The first of these characters represents a self that is constantly on the lookout for chinks in the armor. Any small failing is picked up almost gleefully and is vigorously criticized. The Treasurer represents a self that is stingy. This stinginess goes beyond money and includes his inability to share himself in intimate relationships. Finally, the Lobbyist stands for the self that seeks to pressure others to fit in with his desires and preferences. This self is always looking for a leverage point and, as a consequence, is too often closed to the needs and concerns of others. Mair's therapeutic strategy is to encourage the client to understand these characters or selves as completely as possible and to enact processes for transcending their destructive tendencies. Thus, it may be that he needs to bring his "Prime Minister" into play to deal with the Leader of the Opposition. This is a talented and effective political operative. She is able to counter at least most of the arguments of her opponent, and where there has been failure, she is able to maintain the advantage by putting a positive "spin" on it. But the Leader of the Opposition also has a positive side. As he is not himself in power, he feels a certain freedom in challenging the Treasurer to free up the resources at his disposal (he is not a Conservative Leader of the Opposition!). He will point out the areas of "national life" that will flourish with an injection of "funding." The Lobbyist, finally, needs to renew his acquaintance with a side of himself that he has been out of touch with, namely his ability to be thoughtful and empathetic. Of course, when he does this he will have to resign his job! No room for softness in the world of political lobbying. Working with the various characters or selves in this way contributes to healing and growth.

American psychologists Hazel Markus and Paula Nurius situate the community of the Self in the context of the future.[8] They talk about the selves we can become and they call these "possible selves." Possible selves refer to how we imaginatively construct our future existence. Caught up in a vision of potential selves are the hopes and dreams, along with the fears and anxieties, of a person. A possible self is the ideal self a person dreams of. But it can also be a self she is afraid of becoming.

> The possible selves that are hoped for might include the successful self, the creative self, the rich self, the thin self, or the loved and admired self, whereas the dreaded possible selves could be the alone self, the depressed self, the incompetent self, the alcoholic self, the unemployed self, or the bag lady self.[9]

It is evident that the model of the Self has been reshaped by psychologists in recent times, but with just a little probing we can also find the idea of subselves in the classic psychologies. Indeed, in looking to Freud and Berne we discover some important insights into the dynamics associated with the first of our major concerns, suppression of selves.

FREUD AND BERNE
ON SUPPRESSION OF SELVES

Freud's doctrine of the Self is built around his notion of three central agencies: the id, the ego, and the superego. The id is located in the unconscious. Bubbling below the surface of consciousness is a cauldron of instinctual drives. These drives refer to our basic tendencies to sexual expression and aggression. The superego indicates the ego of another superimposed on a person. That is, we all grow up under the press of the rules, values, and taboos of significant authority figures. At home, in the school, and out in the community we experience ourselves coming under the sway of personal and communal values and preferences. Over time, these powerful voices are internalized to form a superego. The power in these voices is maintained through the weapon of guilt. When we go against the dictates of the superego, we experience strong guilt feelings. Mediating between the press of the id on the one side, and that of the superego on the other, is the ego. It is the executive agency within the psyche. The ego regulates and channels the uncontrolled forces of the id in order to meet the demands of the real world, and it chooses how it will respond to the pressure of the superego.

It is possible, I think, to construe Freud's construction of the Self in terms of three subselves. There is an instinctual self (the id), a civilizing or moralizing self (the superego), and an executive self (the ego). It is not necessary to discuss here all the complexities of the Freudian theory of psychic dysfunction. Rather, to concentrate on just one important dimension of it will, I hope, contribute to our attempt to understand the dynamics of suppression within the Self. This dimension is the relationship between the superego and the ego. A strong ego represents personal freedom and autonomy. When superego voices are particularly strong and the ego relatively weak, however, what might be called the autonomous self is all but forced out of existence. The self that represents deep desires and cherished values may still be part of the community, but its voice is weak and easily silenced. It cannot be heard over the thundering of the superego voices. Consider the case of a married woman whose children are now at school. She enjoyed being at home with them in their preschool years, but is currently contemplating reestablishing herself in her career. She considers the possibility of a postgraduate course at a university. But in the process of thinking about this possibility, she finds herself feeling very guilty. The superego has launched itself and is telling her that it is wrong for her to reenter the professional world because to do so would constitute a failure to honor her responsibilities as mother and as wife. If the superego is powerful enough, she will cut off the professional self and live through her family self. She may even attempt to convince herself that this professional self is not a particularly important part of her personhood. Because it is in fact strongly defining of her Self, the price she will pay in terms of her emotional well-being will be very high. Integration within the community of the Self is only possible if the executive self or ego can be strengthened sufficiently to break the tyrannical hold of the superego.

There are similarities between Freud's theory and the P-A-C theory of Eric Berne. The P-A-C construction is the foundational theory in Transactional Analysis. Berne construes the Self in terms of three "ego states": the Parent, the Adult, and the Child. The Parent, as we shall see in more detail later, represents the internalization of parental injunctions, rules, and values. It is thus similar to the idea of the superego. Further, the Adult, also to be discussed more fully later, has an executive function in relation to the other ego states and can therefore be linked to Freud's ego. I would not want, however, to push these connections too far. There are similarities, but there are also significant differences.[10]

Berne first began to think in terms of an "adult," a "child," and a "parent" in the personality in the 1950s. A thirty-five-year-old lawyer in therapy made the comment "I'm not really a lawyer, I'm just a little boy."[11] Berne began to theorize that all of us have a little child within, and that sometimes this child moves to center stage in the way we relate to others. The adult dimension in the personality is put out of commission for a time and the child takes over. Later, he would add in the idea that along with the child and the adult, there is also a parental dimension in the personality.

During the first five or so years of a life a child records a whole host of experiences and events which produce in her a Parent and a Child. Through the moral and practical teaching of her mother and father her Parent develops. She records on her Parental tape all the rules, laws, and ideas—the way of viewing the world and living in it—of her parents. The Child is expressive of that part of a person that is at times playful, creative, and intuitive, and at other times conforming or rebellious. All infants must endure the civilizing process. During this training, all kinds of feelings are evoked. Perhaps the dominant ones are frustration and failure. The child, for example, wants to carry out bodily functions with complete freedom, but Mom and Dad insist on the use of the toilet and are quick to chastise when it is not used. Through the battle of wills the Child develops, which in some cases is predominantly conforming and in others predominantly rebellious. The bright side of growing up is that children make all kinds of wonderful discoveries. In these discoveries, the powers of intuition and creativity are activated and take up residence in the Child.

The Adult, finally, is the "computer" that receives data from the Parent and the Child on the one hand, and from the outside world on the other, and processes it. It is reality based. An important function of the Adult is to decide whether or not the information in the Parent and the feelings in the Child are still appropriate in the current situation.

The role of the Adult is to discern whether input from the other two ego states is appropriate. If, for example, you are standing before an authority figure feeling quite small and insignificant you know that your Child is "hooked." The Adult can be mobilized and you will say to yourself, "Hang on. I'm an adult and I can relate as an equal to this person. I don't need to be so deferential." Or if you find yourself living the same pattern of workaholism as your father (your Parent says that life begins and ends with effort and achievement), you might want to use your rational facility to ask whether this is something you consciously and freely choose.

It is evident, then, that in P-A-C theory we find a community of selves: a taught self, a thinking self, and a feeling self. What can this theory teach us about the way selves are suppressed? First, there seems to be within Berne's theory a description of a dynamic similar to Freud's superego-ego struggle. Parental voices, when sufficiently strong, can result in a decommissioning of the Adult. The Adult wants to lead the person in the direction of her cherished values, dreams, and hopes, but the Parent wins out and she finds herself holding down a number of possible selves. The "green" self gets very little play in her life ("Environmentalists are soft-headed nuts"). Suppressed also is the progressive self ("Stick with the tried and true"). Finally, the creative self is held down ("Arty people are so flighty and out of touch"). A strong Adult is required for a person to give expression to her full range of selves.

We saw above that the Child is expressive of both conformity and freedom (in the sense of spontaneity, playfulness, and creativity). Indeed, in a development in the basic P-A-C theory, Berne began to work with the concepts of the Adapted Child and the Natural or Free Child.[12] For many of us, conformity becomes a powerful factor in our lives. We find ourselves controlled by a host of internalized "shoulds" and "oughts." Thinking that we are simply being sensible and responsible, we don't stop long enough to reflect on what has happened to us. What has happened is that we have cut off the self that is enlivened by spontaneity and playfulness. We are so busy being sensible that much of the vitality and joy of life has seeped out of us. When the Free Child begins to press into our lives, it is quickly forced down.

SUPPRESSION OF SELVES
AND THE CHRISTIAN LIFE

It is perhaps not too difficult to identify the selves that are commonly held down by Christians. We only need look to the rules and principles that shape church culture (the taught self at work) to find the clues. Here are some of the popular ones:

> Anger is bad; niceness is good.
> Busyness is good; it shows real commitment.
> Doubt has no place in the life of the Christian.
> Conservative is good; radical is bad.

I'm sure you could add a dozen more to the list. If we internalize these rules, we will find that certain selves that need expression are held down. The angry self, the fun self, the doubting self, and the radical self—along with many other selves—will be constantly kept in check and our physical, emotional, and spiritual well-being will suffer significantly as a result. Let me illustrate this process of suppression through the experiences of Nellie and Dan (Nellie I knew in the past and have no contact with now; Dan is a close friend).

Nellie is the chairperson of her church council. For the most part, she is a placid and easygoing person. She finds that she can work well with most people. She values cooperation and appreciates the need for flexibility and openness in working relationships. But like all of us, there are times when Nellie gets really cross with some of the people she shares leadership with. There are two or three members of the church council who sometimes act quite inappropriately. They have a tendency to make personal attacks and to use threats when the discussion is swinging away from them. On occasion, she really feels like expressing her anger, but something holds her back. If she were to reflect on it for a moment, she might become aware of how deeply embedded in "the culture of niceness" she is. She is profoundly afraid of getting mad and showing another (in church circles, unacceptable) side of herself. The angry self, a valid expression of her selfhood, is constantly suppressed. To be sure, there is a payoff for her. She is often complimented for her calm and gracious style. But Nellie knows that she is paying a high price for holding down the angry self. When she goes home after a bad meeting, she "stews" over what those #@@%* said. The scenario at the meeting runs through her head over and over and she finds herself sinking into a depressed state.

In recent times, Dan has been working harder and harder for his local church. He is the treasurer and a member of the church council, the chair of the property and finance committee, and has recently taken on a role as leader of his Bible study group. Most nights of the week Dan is out at a church meeting or activity. As in the case of Nellie, there is a payoff. Others in the congregation (with the exception of his wife and children) are suitably impressed: "Dan is so incredibly committed." "Doesn't Dan do a fantastic job?" "If more people were like Dan this church would really be going places." Of course, there is also a cost. His wife and children are very disappointed that they don't see more of him. He works full-time in paid employment and with all the extra commitments is feeling quite jaded. He is losing his sense of humor; life has become deadly serious for him. He is constantly tired and too often finds himself being snappy with the members of his family. His personal friendships are suffering. I phoned him once to make a date for our families to get together. In fact, over the course of a year we made several dates. But each time he cancelled. "Don't be too disappointed with me," he would say, "but we need to find another time. I won't be able to enjoy getting together with all the stuff I've got hanging over my head." I responded by pointing out how unhealthy this pattern is. But he couldn't hear me. Dan has a compulsion to be busy, to be achieving goals. In his discipleship the same dynamic is at work. The self that wants to achieve constantly pushes down the self that wants to have some fun and to nurture personal relationships.

How can people such as Nellie and Dan free up the selves they are holding down? Nothing can be achieved unless the suppression is acknowledged. Nellie was able to do this. She was able to see that her exaggerated fear of conflict was preventing her from appropriately expressing the anger she was feeling. Unfortunately, the same cannot be said of Dan. He has lost contact with that side of him that really values quality time spent with others and enjoying life. Until he reaches the point of saying "I want my life back," there is no possibility of him unchaining himself from his busyness.

Trusted friends and colleagues play an important role. They can advocate for the suppressed self or selves. I really want to help Dan get some balance back in his life. Dan's relational self and his fun self need to reestablish themselves. At this point in time I am not having much success. Dan's Self must come to the point of accepting that it really needs the suppressed selves to be alive and well. I haven't given up; it's just that I'm having real difficulty finding a way to help Dan free himself from the stranglehold of his overachiever self.

Friends can also give permission for a subself to become more active. Nellie needs to hear that it is okay for the angry self to come out sometimes. She is afraid, however, that if she cuts it any slack she will lose control and "blast" others. She has to keep it on a tight rein, she thinks. What she needs to hear is that there is a greater likelihood of her losing control if she continues to keep the angry self reined in. There may well come a time when there is a "spontaneous combustion." The angry self will burst out explosively and wreak havoc. It is much better for her to let it constructively express itself each and every time it feels a need.

How in general terms can we characterize the attitude that Nellie and Dan have toward their suppressed selves? Is it an attitude of liking or of disliking? Or is it something else again? Dan likes his fun and social selves, although sometimes he resents them pressing in on his need to get more work done. Nellie, on the other hand, seems to dislike her angry self because she is frightened of it. She is frightened that it will take over.

Looking in from the outside at Nellie, one could say that though she may feel uncomfortable about the angry self and the possibility of it exploding out, she does not need to see it as inferior or weak. Anger is a valid emotion. There are other selves, however, in Dan and in Nellie, or in anyone else for that matter, that are experienced as inferiorities. It is these selves that get disowned. As in the case of suppression, I will call on two of the classic psychological theorists to shed light for us. Heinz Kohut and Carl Jung offer interesting and enlightening interpretations of the process of isolating subselves.

KOHUT AND JUNG ON DISOWNING SELVES

Heinz Kohut can be located within the Freudian school of psychotherapy. Throughout his career he wanted to maintain contact with the psychoanalytic tradition. However, as his theory of the self developed, central Freudian planks such as the unconscious and the three mental agencies—id, ego, and superego—receded into the background. He is usually referred to as neo-Freudian (he uses some Freudian concepts but he takes them in a new direction).

Marie Hoskins and Johanna Leseho argue that Kohut and his concept of the "cohesive self" is representative of the older approach to selfhood.[13] Here, they suggest, is a model of selfhood built around the notion of a unitary self. It is true that Kohut understands the Self in terms of a personal core; it is "a center of productive initiative."[14] This Self is superordinate to the mental agencies (id, ego, and superego).[15] Nevertheless, the Self is also understood by Kohut as a community. The smallest form of community is a couple. What Kohut calls the "bipolar self" accounts for two basic psychological functions: healthy self-assertiveness in relation to the mother (usually) who "mirrors" it, reflects it back, and affirming and healthy admiration for the father (usually).[16] Thus it is possible, theorizes Kohut, to identify a *grandiose self* that seeks admiration and approval, and an *idealizing self* that aims at identification with an admired other. The grandiose self wants to have its talents, abilities, and achievements affirmed and valued. The idealizing self seeks to merge with the significant other whose ideals, goals, and ambitions are valued. When these two basic psychological needs for admiration and merger are fulfilled in infantile development, a "cohesive self" emerges. Put it simply, what a child needs most is to admire and to be admired. If these needs are met through "good enough parenting" (to use Donald Winnicott's expression), the self will achieve wholeness or cohesion.

Kohut observes that there is often trouble in this tiny community. The two selves find themselves at enmity with each other. Kohut describes the strife through a reference to shame. Though he does not use the actual word very often, his work is filled with cognate terms such as low self-esteem, embarrassment, and inferiority feelings. Now either the grandiose or the idealizing self may experience shame, depending on the circumstances. A faux pas is an example of the grandiose self experiencing shame. A Bible study leader, for instance, has been trying to impress a group with the depth of his biblical knowledge and, embarrassingly, a member of the group exposes some significant errors in his account of a story.

When, on the other hand, a person's actual performance is judged to be below the standard established as ideal, the idealizing self is the locus of shame. A person is asked to make an important presentation at work. She prepares long and hard because she wants her work to be well received. As she is giving her presentation, though, she senses that she is missing the target. There is a gap between the ideal she has set and her actual performance.

Whether it is the grandiose or the idealizing self that experiences shame, the end result is the same: an experience of painful disharmony in the relationship between the two selves. This disharmony is the result of the grandiose self rejecting the idealizing self, and vice versa. What is required is reconciliation between the two selves. The trouble comes because each self tends to be overly critical and harsh in relation to the other. Kohut's solution is "mirroring" (or admiration and approval). That is, the selves need to learn to value and affirm each other rather than constantly being critical and condemning.

As with the other classic constructions of the Self, I believe a communitarian dimension is clearly present in the thought of C. G. Jung. Jung was at one time the "chosen one" in the Freudian school. Freud saw him as his natural successor. However, Jung found himself disagreeing with his mentor in relation to two central theoretical areas, namely, the interpretation of dreams and the role of sex in psychic energy (libido). Freud could not tolerate such dissension, and an acrimonious split followed.

Jung refers to the three archetypes (inherited psychic paradigms or models) "which have the most frequent and the most disturbing influence on the ego" as the anima, the animus, and the shadow.[17] The anima and the animus (the syzygy) belong to the collective unconscious. That is, we receive them not through our personal mental history but through our connection with the collective psychological, cultural, and spiritual experience of humankind. Since the anima and the animus come to us through the collective experience of humanity, they have a certain autonomy in their engagement with the ego (the agent of consciousness in the psyche). The shadow, on the other hand, though it may sometimes arise from the collective unconscious, is usually located in the personal unconscious.

The animus is the "masculine imprint" on the female psyche. It is derived from the Logos (mind, rationality). The "feminine imprint" in the male is the anima. Here there is a connection with Eros (relationality). It is not possible, however, to give these two concepts too precise a definition. Jung puts it this way:

> I use Eros and Logos merely as conceptual aids to describe the fact that woman's consciousness is characterized more by the connective quality of Eros than by the discrimination and cognition associated with Logos. In men, Eros, the function of relationship, is usually less developed than Logos. In women, on the other hand, Eros is an expression of their true nature, while their Logos is often only a regrettable accident.[18]

Jung is a child of his time and gender stereotyping is evident in his formulation of the syzygy. Leaving this concern aside just for a moment, what we have in Jungian thought are two selves that are present in each person: a feminine or relational self and a masculine or logical/rational self. For our time, though, it is necessary to question the use of the masculine and feminine labels. Having said that, it does seem to be the case, and this comes out quite strongly in feminist writings, that relationality and connectiveness are strengths within women. But to link rationality and logic so strongly with masculinity is inappropriate. Now that women feel freer to enter fields of endeavor grounded in mathematics and the sciences, there is ample evidence that they are doing at least as well as, if not better than, men.

However the issue of gender labeling is to be resolved, what is important for psychological integration is that neither self is disowned. While, as I have just said, feminism has resulted in many more women readily embracing their logical/thinking side, there are still those women who disown it. Perhaps they undervalue a capacity for rational/logical processes, or lack confidence in this capacity, or it may be that they remain ensnared in the myth that thinking hard doesn't fit with being feminine. There are many men, on the other hand, who are able to connect with their relational self, but even in these days of sensitive New Age guys, there are many who define themselves almost completely in terms of tasks and achievements. There is clearly wisdom in Jung's exhortation to own and integrate the Eros and the Logos selves.

The shadow refers to "the dark aspects of the personality."[19] These "inferiorities" have an *"emotional* nature, a kind of autonomy, and accordingly an obsessive or, better, possessive quality."[20] Here, then, is the danger associated with the shadow. A person can become a passive victim of his unconscious emotional life. "Salvation" comes through self-awareness. But of course this dark self is exceedingly difficult to get in touch with. To acknowledge our inferiorities is to experience a heavy assault on our self-esteem. Consequently, the shadow self is very often disowned. And when it is disowned, it is projected onto others. "Projections change the world into the replica of one's unknown face."[21] So not only do we suffer under the sway of powerful affects, we also damage our interpersonal life through projection. Owning the dark self is thus a moral imperative.

WORKING WITH DISOWNED SUBSELVES

John Bradshaw is a therapist who also had theological training. He has concentrated on his work and writing on the problem of shame. Although I will need to challenge Bradshaw's view that all of our selves are "okay," I do find his strategies for integrating disowned selves quite helpful.[22] I will present just two of these (the others involve dream work and would involve us in technicalities beyond the scope of this chapter). The first is called "Making Peace with All Your Villagers" (it is a modified version of an approach used by therapists Hal Stone and Sidra Winkelman). The starting point in this strategy is calling to mind all the people you dislike (the person you have the strongest negative feelings about goes to the top of the list). Then you attempt to identify the reprehensible traits in each person. Now you ask yourself: What is the one trait that brings out feelings of righteousness and goodness most strongly in me? The final step is to choose the one most despicable trait for each person. Bradshaw supplies an example:

a. Joe Slunk—Grandiose egomaniac
b. Gwendella Farboduster—Aggressive and rude
c. Maximillian Quartz—Hypocrite (Pretends to help people; does it for money)
d. Farquahr Evenhouser—Uses Christian facade to cover up phoniness
e. Rothghar Pieopia—A wimp; has no mind of his own[23]

Bradshaw suggests that each of these personality traits represents a disowned self. Here he is working with Jung's shadow theory. Not wanting to integrate a particular "energy pattern" into your Self, he says, you externalize it. That is, the disowned personality trait is projected; your shadow shows up in "the five most hated" list.

These people on the list can, however, become your teachers. Bradshaw suggests that we engage these people in a dialogue. You can question each person directly: "How do you see life, relationships, God?" Through this conversation you will be able to look at selves that you are "overidentified" with. The result, says Bradshaw, will be very positive: "You may be surprised at the new energy you receive from this exercise. You are bringing a part of you out of hiding and secrecy. You are turning your shadow into light."[24] The question is: What do you do with the "part" when it is in the light? I suggest that when the part or self is acknowledged not only does it need love and acceptance, it also needs reformation. This will be discussed more fully later.

The second and final strategy of Bradshaw's that we will look at (based on the work by leading family therapist Virginia Satir) is called "The Parts Party."[25] Here he does acknowledge the need for modifying selves that are hindering a person. A theatrical setting is used here. You are invited to imagine yourself presenting a "review" of your subselves. You begin by thinking of a part of yourself that you really like, and then you connect it with a famous person who will enter the stage. "I like my humor," says Bradshaw, "and I see Johnny Carson walk out." And as your famous person walks out, you hear the applause. This exercise is repeated four times so that you now have five famous people out on stage in celebration of your positive side. But there is, of course, a shadow to deal with. So you invite five people out representing subselves you dislike. And as you do, you hear a loud boo from the imaginary audience. Now comes the healing action within this "Parts Party":

> [I]magine that a wise and beautiful person walks to the center of the stage. This person can look like an old man with a beard or a radiant youth like Jesus or a warm nurturing mother or whatever. . . . Just let your wise person appear. . . . Then see her walking off the stage and coming to get you. . . . As she approaches, notice whatever strikes you about her. . . . Then hear her invite you to come up on the stage and review your many parts. Walk around each person who represents a part of you; look her in the face. How does each part help you? How does each part hinder or limit you, especially your undesirable parts? What can you learn from your undesirable parts? What can they teach you? Now imagine they are all interacting. Imagine them at a table discussing a problem. Think of a current problem you have. What does your humor say about that? How is that helpful? How does it hinder you? How does your disorganization help you? What would happen if you simply didn't have this part? What would you lose? How would you like to change the part you want to reject? Modify that part in the way it would be more beneficial. . . . How does it feel to modify that part?. . . Now go around and repeat that procedure with every single part. Modify it until it feels right for you. Then walk up to each part and imagine that part melting into you. Do this until you are alone on the stage with your wise person. Hear the wise person tell you that this is the theater of your life.[26]

Exercises such as these can be most helpful in the task of reclaiming disowned selves. But in encountering approaches such as these, oriented as they are to boosting self-acceptance and self-esteem, I find myself wondering whether sufficient emphasis is given to the moral dimension in the life of the community of the Self. Certainly Jung was keenly aware of the need for such an emphasis:

> The shadow is a moral problem that challenges the whole ego-personality, for no one can become conscious of the shadow without considerable moral effort. To become conscious of it involves recognizing the dark aspects of the personality as present and real. This act is the essential condition for any kind of self-knowledge, and it therefore, as a rule, meets with considerable resistance.[27]

Bradshaw seems not to have this same depth of insight. It is true that in his exercises he identifies morally inadequate characters. It is also true that he refers to the need to modify subselves that may be hindering us. But at the same time he can happily embrace the guiding principle advocated by Stone and Winkelman:[28]

> [A]*ll of our parts are okay.* Nothing could be more affirming and less shaming. Every aspect of every person is crucial for wholeness and completeness. There is no law which says that one part is better than another part. Our consciousness with its many selves needs to operate on principles of social equality and democracy.[29] (emphasis in the original)

Is it really true to say that all our subselves are "okay"? Surely if a person has a dark self that is hurting both herself and those around her, that is not okay.

Although Kohut advocates an unconditional prizing of the two principal selves, I do not have the same concern with his approach. His theory relates especially to the shame that is associated with a failure to feel a sense of achievement. Recall that his grandiose self is connected with talents and abilities, and his idealizing self with goals and ambitions. Rather than being condemning over failures, he argues, the selves should mirror each other. This approval and admiration refers to the morally neutral area of competence. A distinction between morally neutral and morally relevant selves is important if we are to get beyond blanket statements about the acceptability of every part of the Self.

MORALLY RELEVANT SELVES

To help us in this task, I propose three places in which we can locate the variety of selves that we all live with: *competence, spirituality,* and *personality.* This list is not intended to be exhaustive; however, it will suffice to indicate the process of distinguishing morally relevant selves from morally neutral ones.

Competence, first, refers to talents, abilities, and achievements. We all have our strengths, and we all struggle in certain areas. Some of us are great with language, but anything to do with mathematics—or even more frightening, computers—leaves us feeling totally incompetent. Others of us revel in figures and problem solving, but are at a loss when we are anywhere near a kitchen. Still others excel on the sports field and are good with most intellectual tasks, but are "all thumbs" when it comes to home maintenance. So there are mathematical selves, computer selves, linguistic selves, culinary selves, sporting selves, and "handy" selves—to nominate just a few areas in which some people are particularly competent. Clearly, we are in an area that is morally neutral. If I burn the roast I have not committed a moral transgression. The fact that I can never remember my eight times table should not be counted against me as sin. We all have our areas of gifting, and we all have areas that are weak. There is no question of interpreting this fact in a moral context.

The second category, *spirituality,* is also morally neutral. We all express our spiritual self differently. There are any number of styles and techniques advocated by those who specialize in the area of spirituality. Some of these we will connect strongly with, and others hardly at all. Here there needs to be, in Bradshaw's terminology, a "principle of social equality." It is not a matter of identifying "the higher way," but rather of finding a way that is personally meaningful and helpful. It may be, for example, that I am attracted to charismatic spirituality. Others feel drawn to a quieter, more contemplative, approach to the spiritual life. There is no reason for me to feel that my charismatic self is either better or worse than someone else's contemplative self.

To be sure, I can be lazy and undisciplined in my spiritual life. At that point a moral concern seems to arise. But the lack of discipline is almost certainly a factor in other areas of my life. That is, it is a personality trait, and we have entered our third and final area.

Under the rubric of *personality,* I include the traits, attitudes, and behaviors that are defining of one's personhood. There are introverts and extroverts, passive aggressives and active aggressives, optimists and pessimists, liberals and conservatives, the patient and the impatient, the hardworking and the slothful, the rash and the prudent, the intimate and the distant, the passionate and the "cool," the self-aware and the unaware, and so on.

Personality traits become especially important in the context of relationships. Our style of relating is determined by our personality. Factors such as the way we deal with anger, our capacity for openness and honesty, our negotiating style, the level of our self-esteem, and our capacity for intimacy are highly significant in the context of interpersonal life. It will be evident that in discussing personality traits and relationality we have entered a morally relevant zone. Our personal failings cause harm to relationships and to the people involved in those relationships. To acknowledge those subselves that wreak havoc in our relationships and to take action on them is a moral imperative.

Let me illustrate these observations through reference to a personal experience.

Jim was a prominent leader in my congregation. He had many admirable qualities. He was hardworking, intelligent, perceptive, reliable, a good listener, and had a strong faith. But most of us on the leadership team found Jim almost impossible to work with. I believe that the problems we encountered had their source in the expression of two selves within Jim: a perfectionist self and a controlling self. "Perfectionist Jim" had to have every "i" dotted and every "t" crossed. If we set up a new program in the congregation, Jim would want a manual covering every possible issue and outlining every conceivable area of responsibility, every conceivable task. He would seek to generate forms for participants to fill in so that every move made could be duly noted and recorded. Jim's preference would be for ten three-hour training sessions for leaders in the program. "If we are going to run this program," Jim would say, "we're going to do it right." To which we would respond, "Well, yes, Jim, we want to do it right, but isn't this just a bit excessive?"

At that point Jim's controlling self would rise up. He could not accept the possibility that any other view was valid. We were simply being "slaphappy" and it was up to him to make sure that things were done properly. He would go on the offensive and seek to control others through aggression. There were enough leaders prepared to agree in order to save themselves from a tongue-lashing that his strategy was most often a successful one. So we lived with the huge manual, the endless forms, and the unrealistic expectations on leaders.

Finding the situation intolerable, I spoke long and hard with Jim on a number of occasions. Looking back on the frustration of not being heard, Jung's words have never sounded more true: Recognizing the shadow "is an essential condition for any kind of self-knowledge, and it therefore, as a rule, meets with considerable resistance."[30] Yes, Carl, I did meet with large amounts of resistance! In Jim's eyes, he was responsible and conscientious, and everyone else was lazy and sloppy. One evening at an informal service the strength of Jim's resistance was brought home to me in a most forceful way. In breaking open the scripture passage, I asked the group to reflect on what trust meant for them. Jim responded with this comment: "I trust no one because everyone lets you down. I have come to trust only God." Hearing that, I felt deeply saddened.

But that is not the end of the story. In the course of our intense discussions, Jim introduced me to my shadow—albeit in a less than desirable way. I had tended to pride myself on my flexibility and openness to the views of others. Jim, however, did not see it that way. He saw me as simply weak and dishonest. At the time, I was exceedingly angry and felt deeply affronted. His comments seemed most unfair, and for a very long time I rejected them out of hand. But there came a time when I found myself pondering the possibility that tied in with his harsh judgment on me there might be a measure of truth. I resisted this idea initially; it was just too painful to face. But slowly it began to dawn on me that behind my open and agreeable nature there lurked a less than noble self. This is the self that is uncomfortable with conflict and tends to agree too readily in the hope of warding it off. This compliant self holds me back from feeling too deeply, from becoming too passionate, because where there is passion conflict is not too far away. Opening myself to God's grace, I have tried to work on changing this side of my personality. To my surprise, the experience of allowing myself to feel deeply and to communicate that to others has been very liberating.

THE SPIRIT AND THE CHRISTIAN'S MORAL IMPERATIVE

I said that the recognition of the shadow side, along with an attempt to reform it, constitutes a moral imperative. Christians have a responsibility to deal with the personality flaws that mitigate constructive relationality. All of us, however, find this task an extremely difficult one (the experiences of both Jim and myself, each in their own ways, witness to this fact). There are a number of reasons for this; I'd like to concentrate on two of the more prominent ones. The first is that a recognition of the shadow side constitutes an assault on our self-esteem. To accept that we have traits that others find annoying, frustrating, or even offensive really hurts. Thus, the tendency to resist acknowledging the shadow side is strong. The second reason that we deny the presence of the dark side, or at least manage to convince ourselves that it is not a serious problem for us, is that change is hard work. It is much easier to coast along in our old patterns than to establish new ones. I want to point to the Spirit of Christ as an enabling power in the change process. The Spirit is available to counter our fears and our apathy.

We are afraid of the pain of acknowledging our less than noble selves. Our sense of self-worth is not so strong that we can readily face our inferiorities. Clearly, if we are to grow we have to find the strength and the courage to face the downward pressure on our self-esteem that comes with owning our shadow selves. The Spirit comes to us in our fear and distress and leads us into the gracious embrace of God the Maker and of Jesus the Redeemer. God's grace is God's loving acceptance. God in Christ speaks a healing and hopeful word: "Despite everything, you are loved and valued." The shadow does not keep God's loving arms at a distance. The father in the story of the prodigal (Lk 15:11-32) knows all about the inferiorities of his son, but on seeing him returning runs to bear-hug him. The Holy Spirit prepares our spirits so that we can open ourselves to God's loving, healing embrace.

I want to also connect the enabling power of the Spirit with the problem of apathy. When we are feeling that change is too demanding, when the temptation to coast is almost overpowering, the Spirit sparks our better intentions. The desire to grow may be like a flickering flame. When we encounter the difficulties associated with the change process, it is in danger of being snuffed out altogether. The Spirit fans that little flame into a fire. If we are fully open to the grace of God, we will become passionate about self-renewal. We want to allow God into the dark places so that we can conform ourselves more closely to Christ.

All of this assumes a capacity to open ourselves to the power of the Spirit. If our sense of self-worth is too fragile, if our commitment to growing psychologically and spiritually is barely in place, we may block the work of the Spirit. But if, on the other hand, we allow space for this work, the burden of change is significantly lightened.

SUMMARY

There is within the Self a community of selves. Some of those selves we suppress because we are controlled by unhealthy inner voices. We hear warnings against the angry self, the fun self, the vulnerable self, and the radical self, to name just a few. We need to find the strength and the confidence to lift the lid on these valid expressions of the Self. Here trusted friends and colleagues play an important role. They can act as advocates for these suppressed selves.

There are also selves that are inferior and that we strongly dislike. Because they cause us a great deal of distress, we disown them. It is common for therapists to tell us that we need to embrace all our selves, that they are all "okay." Certainly every subself needs our love and acceptance. But it is not appropriate to turn a blind eye to the moral dimension in the life of the Self. If there is a self that is damaging us, our relationships, and other people, it is not an "okay" self. We need to develop an awareness of its nature and the dynamics associated with the harm it does. And we need to take steps to reform this wayward self. This is no easy task. Fear and apathy block our good intentions. The Holy Spirit is available to us as an enabling power that breaks through these roadblocks.

Chapter 3

Wholeness, Not Perfection

In the previous chapter, I highlighted the importance of attempting to reform shadow selves. The subselves that adversely affect both our personal well-being and our relationships with others need to be challenged and improved. But herein lies a danger. Intent on maximizing our moral improvement, we may unwittingly fall into an unhealthy perfectionism. We recall the words of Jesus: "You must be perfect, just as your heavenly Father is perfect" (Mt 5:48), and find ourselves setting impossible goals for ourselves. Pathology sets in; we are constantly plagued by an inappropriate sense of failure and guilt.

If we are to avoid this pathology, we need to aim for completeness rather than perfection. This all-important distinction is one that is developed by Carl Jung. Perfection, he observes, belongs only to God; the goal of self-realization (or "individuation") is completeness or wholeness. Realization of the self is not established through a complete victory over the shadow side, but rather through achieving reconciliation with it. For Jung, a reconciliation of opposites is most fully demonstrated in Christ. Indeed, he holds up Christ as the symbol of the Self (the capital "S" indicates a specific psychic agency or archetype whose task it is to promote wholeness). But in this context it is not the perfection in the Christ archetype that is primary, but rather its completeness. The totality of the symbol is revealed in the reconciliation within Christ of the unitemporal (the humanity of Christ) and the eternal (his divinity), of the unique and the individual, of the spiritual and the material, and of good and evil (the sinless one opposed by the Antichrist).

Moving Toward Spiritual Maturity
© 2007 by The Haworth Press, Inc. All rights reserved.
doi:10.1300/5886_03

Significantly, Jung also points to the hubris of positing the reverse relationship between the Self and Christ. When we seek to make the Self the archetype of Christ, we fall into a terrible tension. We are forced toward a goal that is simply impossible, namely the perfection of Christ.

Jung contends that in striving for moral perfection a person will inevitably be caught up in an intense inner struggle. He uses Paul's reflections in Romans 7 to make his point: "I don't do the good I want to; instead, I do the evil that I do not want to do." Jung's point is that a one-sided focus on goodness results in a backlash from the shadow side. The shadow rises up in protest when it is not given its due. I will be arguing, though, that he misreads Paul here. Paul is not an advocate for moral perfection. Indeed, the clear implication of the Romans 7 text is that aiming for perfect goodness is futile. We will inevitably fall short of moral perfection because of the power of the law of sin. Try as we might to kick the shadow out, it simply will not budge.

I will also be suggesting that we need to move beyond psychological categories if we are to fully understand the nature of wholeness. Paul's understanding of the human condition does not begin and end with the struggle, with the tension. In verse 24 he asks, "Who will rescue me from this body of death?" And the answer comes, "Thanks be to God—through Jesus Christ our Lord!" The saving grace, literally, for Paul is that in Christ and the reconciliation he has won for us we experience complete healing. The point that I will be making, then, is that the reconciliation of inner opposites can only ever be a provisional experience of wholeness; only in God's future will we know the true meaning of psychospiritual completeness.

THE BIND OF PERFECTIONISM

In the previous chapter, I questioned John Bradshaw's counsel that we should feel free to view all our subselves as "okay." You will recall that he also suggests that there needs to be a "social equality" at work: no subself should be considered better than any other. I agreed with him that each and every self needs to be accepted, but I challenged his view that each and every one is acceptable. Once we begin to think in terms of morally relevant selves, such a position is clearly inappropriate. A courageous self seems better than an arrogant self, and with reference to the latter a person is under a moral imperative to mitigate her arrogant tendencies.

I am aware that contained in a stress on the need for moral improvement is the risk of perfectionism. One might say that for the Christian this risk goes with the territory. In our tradition we have been exhorted to imitate the one who was without sin. When we engage with those outside the church we sometimes feel the pressure in a particularly acute way. We go as Jesus' ambassadors and we may feel that we need to be *alter Christus*. It is a good thing to strive for a consistent and strong witness to God's love. But our mental and spiritual health will suffer if we compulsively strive after impossibly high goals. At every turn we will be plagued by a deep sense of failure and by the accompanying guilt. The befriending voice of God is there— "You are loved by me, precious in my sight"—but it is drowned out by the chorus of superego voices. We are attacked by messages such as these: "You should be better than that"; "You're a poor excuse for a Christian"; and "You should practice what you preach." We find ourselves under "the tyranny of the shoulds" (Karen Horney).

Now of course some will say that Jesus himself sets before us an ideal that is always beyond our reach: "You must therefore be perfect, just as your heavenly Father is perfect" (Mt 5:48). The logic, they suggest, is that even though we cannot hope to attain perfection, we should still be striving for it. It is important, then, to inquire as to exactly what is meant in this text. As always, it's helpful to set the verse in context. In this part of the Sermon on the Mount, Jesus is exhorting his followers to extend their love beyond their friends to their enemies: "You have heard how it was said, You will love your neighbor and hate your enemy. But I say this to you, love your enemies and pray for those who persecute you; so that you may be children of your Father in heaven . . ." (vv. 43-45a). We become children of God when we reflect God's universal love. God's sun shines on the wicked and the righteous alike, and God's rain is similarly impartial. We are called, then, to an impartial love. But our call is to completeness rather than perfection. As scripture scholar J. Andrew Overman points out, we should not in fact render the Greek word used in the text, *teleioi*, as "perfect" but rather as "complete."[1] To be complete as God is complete is to love one's enemies. "The fulfillment of the law and the goal of reiterating within the Matthean community the fullness and righteousness of the heavenly kingdom are accomplished through the enactment of the love command in the relationships and conflict the community encounters."[2]

Even if we grant that this is not a counsel of perfection but rather a call to completeness through impartial love, the danger of perfectionism is not removed. We can certainly become perfectionistic in our striving to love our enemies! We will always fall short in this incredibly difficult calling. Though in general we are loving persons, there will be within most of us a subself who hates the enemy and is calling out for revenge. There is plenty of scope here for excessive self-criticism. At this point I believe that Jung's concept of individuation is helpful in gaining perspective. The goal of self-realization is not perfection in love but rather reconciliation between inner opposites. The self that is striving to love the enemy and the shadow self that is hell bent on revenge need to acknowledge each other and to work together in promoting psychic wholeness.

CHRIST AND INDIVIDUATION

"Individuation" is the term Jung uses to denote the process of embracing one's "innermost, last and incomparable uniqueness."[3] That is, it concerns realizing the self that one truly is. There is, however, a constant temptation to bypass the demanding personal work that this involves. Instead of coming to terms with the real self, a person falls into "alienations of the self."[4] She lives through her persona or through the generic symbols thrown up by the collective unconscious rather than through a genuine encounter with her "incomparable uniqueness." This genuine encounter involves a reconciliation of opposites: persona and shadow, male and female aspects. Jung embraces the ancient wisdom that locates completeness or totality in the balancing of opposites. Time and again he identifies the quaternions of opposites (fourfold patterns of opposition) that symbolize totality (e.g., the four corners of the Earth, the Great Spirit at the center of a circle divided into four, the four seasons of the sun in the circle of the Zodiac, etc.).

I did introduce some Jungian concepts in the previous chapter. However, in case the reader is not very familiar with the Jungian approach, I will lay out the fundamentals[5] before proceeding with a discussion of his approach to the relationship between Christ and individuation. Let me begin with Jung's term, namely *psyche*.

Jung uses the term *psyche* to refer to the personality as a whole. It's a Latin word meaning "soul" or "spirit," but today it is usually taken to mean "mind." When we refer to "psychology" we are using it in this latter way. Included within the provenance of the psyche are all thought, feeling, and behavior, and these aspects of human experience operate on both conscious and unconscious levels.

Other psychological theorists construe the personality as something that starts small and develops over time. Jung, however, asserts that personality is a whole to begin with. Wholeness in the psyche is not the result of a developmental process; rather, it is something that we are born with. In all of us, there is a tendency to lose this wholeness over time. That is, the psyche begins to break up into separate and conflicting systems. Jung's patients were those in whom this splitting of the psyche was severe. His aim in analysis was to help them achieve a higher level of integration or wholeness.

Wholeness is achieved as the consciousness of a person becomes differentiated from that of other people. This process, as we have seen, Jung referred to as individuation. It concerns realizing the self that one truly is. Another way of putting it is to say that it is about knowing oneself as fully as possible, about expanding awareness.

The ego is the term that Jung uses for the organization of consciousness. "We understand the ego," he writes, "as the complex factor to which all conscious contents are related. It forms . . . the center of the field of consciousness, and . . . is the subject of all personal acts of consciousness."[6] The only reason that an idea, feeling, or memory comes into our field of awareness is because it is acknowledged by the ego. If the ego lets everything we experienced in a day into our consciousness we would be swamped. It therefore performs an important screening function.

If some psychic material is screened out, what happens to it? Obviously it does not simply disappear from the psyche; it must exist somewhere. This material, according to Jung, gets stored in the *personal unconscious*. It is the container that holds all the psychic elements that do not fit with conscious needs and desires. On the other hand, it may be that the ego did let a particular idea, issue, or feeling into consciousness, but it caused such distress that it got pushed out of consciousness. This is the process of repression.

The personal unconscious might be thought of as a data storage system—such as we find in a computer. There is a very large amount of information that a person uses every day, but this data does not sit in the conscious mind all the time. Like a computer, a mind needs free space to operate. Files get called up as required. The directory where these files may be found is the personal unconscious.

Experiences that have passed unnoticed during the day, or which have registered only vaguely in the conscious mind, may appear at night in dreams. The personal unconscious is an important source of material for dream images.

Another important feature of the personal unconscious is that various psychic elements may group to form a cluster or constellation. Jung calls these *complexes*. He refers to them as "repressed emotional themes."[7] Jung first began to think in terms of these repressed constellations as a result of his work on word association tests. In these tests, a list of words is read off one at a time and the person is instructed to respond with the first word that comes into his head. Jung observed that sometimes there was a delay in a person's reply. He reasoned that there must be associated groups of feelings and thoughts in the unconscious holding back the person. Jung began to think of these complexes as being like separate subpersonalities. They are autonomous, operate according to their own rules and motivations, and can exert considerable control over a person's thoughts and behavior.

An example of this phenomenon would be the mother complex.[8] The person under the sway of the mother complex cares very much about what his mother says and thinks. Stories, movies, and events in which a mother figure is prominent will be of special interest to him. Events such as Mother's Day and his mother's birthday are particularly important in his calendar because they afford an opportunity to honor her.

When complexes are strong, and possess a destructive theme, neurosis is the result. They get a grip on a person and control her thoughts, feelings, and actions. It is not so much that she has a complex, but rather that the complex has her. A central aim in Jung's analytical therapy is to break up these complexes and thus to set a person free from their power.

Just now I have said that a complex with "a destructive theme" leads to neurosis. It was necessary to put it this way to indicate that not all complexes result in dysfunctional thinking and acting. They can be sources of inspiration and creative endeavor. A complex is sometimes the seat of a creative power that drives a person to great achievements in the arts, humanities, or science.

Jung wondered where these complexes originated. Freud believed that all neurosis had its origin in traumatic experiences in early childhood. In his early reflections, Jung was inclined to follow this approach. Complexes began their life after a distressing childhood experience. So, for example, a child separated from his mother may develop a mother complex later in life. Jung was happy with this theory for a time, but soon began to think that there must be something deeper behind complexes than early childhood experiences. In his thinking about what this might be, he discovered another level in the psyche, and he called this the *collective unconscious*.

In positing the ego as the center of consciousness and the personal unconscious as the container for repressed psychic material, Jung was traversing well-known territory. These were not new ideas in the field of psychology. But the notion that input into the shaping of the mind came from somewhere outside the field of environmental influences was truly original.

What Jung has done with his idea of the archetypes is show that the psyche is part of an evolutionary process, just as the body is. The collective unconscious is a reservoir of "primordial images." These are images that have been passed on by our distant ancestors.

The collective unconscious can be distinguished from the personal unconscious by the fact that its life is independent of personal experience. The material in the personal unconscious was once part of conscious awareness, but the contents of the collective unconscious never come into consciousness in the lifetime of an individual. The images that rise up from the collective unconscious predispose a person to experience life in the same general way that our ancestors did. The images are not specific ideas. So I will not think about life and the world in just the way that an indigenous Australian or African did 50,000 years ago. But the images we share speak to general themes and values in human existence. These images have great power and significance because they relate to needs and desires that are deep within all of us.

Compared to the objective unconscious, the personal dimension of our psychic experience is shallow. Writes Jung:

> Our personal psychology is just a thin skin, a ripple on the ocean of collective psychology. The powerful factor, the factor which changes our whole life, which changes the surface of our known world, which makes history, is collective psychology, and collective psychology moves according to laws entirely different from those of our consciousness. The archetypes are the great decisive forces, they bring about the real events, and not our personal reasoning and practical intellect.[9]

Here we have a reference to the archetypes. These are the contents of the collective unconscious. The word *archetype* means an original model; it is that which other similar things are based on. It has a similar meaning to the word *prototype*.[10]

The archetype should not be identified with certain definite mythological images or motifs, however. These are simply conscious representations, and they vary enormously. How could all of these primordial pictures be passed on? The archetype is not this or that representation—a snake, a heroic leader, a circle—but rather "a tendency to form such representations of a motif."[11] There are many representations of the motif of the hero or the mandala, but the motif remains the same. Jung spent a great deal of his life researching the various archetypes. Among the numerous ones that he identified and described are those of birth, rebirth, death, power, magic, the hero, the child, the trickster, God, the demon, the wise old man, the earth mother, the giant, trees, the sun, the moon, wind, rivers, fire, and animals.

Some archetypes have such a significant effect in shaping personality that Jung gave them a special treatment. These are the *persona,* the *anima* and *animus,* the *shadow,* and the *Self.* It is to a consideration of these central archetypes that we now turn.

The word *persona* originally referred to the mask worn by an actor in a play. Wearing the mask, the actor was able to play a specific role. In Jungian psychology, the word functions in a similar way. The persona archetype allows a person to act out her social and professional roles. She wears her "public face" in order to gain social acceptance.

She knows what is expected of her and through her persona she conforms.

The persona is necessary for survival. It oils the machinery of social interaction. As soon as a person refuses to adopt a persona it creates a level of uncertainty, confusion, and anxiety. I remember a conservative, middle-aged woman telling me about a recent visit to a public hospital. She was suffering from a life-threatening disease and waiting for her first appointment with her doctor. She saw a doctor come out to call a patient. He had a long ponytail, a long beard, and an earring. Her heart sank and she said to her husband, "Don't tell that *he's* going to be my doctor!" Unfortunately, she spoke too loudly and the doctor heard her. "Yes, and aren't you lucky," he said. According to many people, a doctor is expected to look and act a certain way. If he departs significantly from the norm, waves are created. Some patients will have their confidence shaken, and the doctor will have to contend with their need for him or her to prove himself or herself.

We usually wear more than one mask. We have one for work, one for home, and one for the tennis club—to name just some of the more common ones. When we take all these masks together we have our persona.

I have just pointed out that the persona helps us in negotiating the public sphere. But it can also be a liability. If a person allows the role to take over, her ego begins to identify almost totally with this role. Other important parts of her personality will be pushed aside. The ego's identification with the persona is called *inflation*. Playing the role so successfully puffs the persona up. The person begins to overrate her self-importance. But there is of course a deficit associated with this. When the role takes over we begin to define ourselves in terms of how well we carry it out. Failure is inevitable, and when it comes our self-esteem takes a battering.

What is required is for the persona to be deflated. This is no easy task, it goes without saying. For years a person has been defining himself in terms of his roles. Now he is asked to put a pin in what until now has been very dear to him.

Jung calls the persona the "outward face" of the psyche because it is the one we wear in public. The "inward face" he calls the *anima* in males and the *animus* in females. We encountered these concepts in the previous chapter. You will recall that the animus is the "masculine imprint" on the female psyche. It is derived from Logos (mind, rationality). The "feminine imprint" in the male is the anima. Here there is a connection with Eros (relationality).

The anima and the animus play a central role in the dynamics of human attraction. We carry within us an image of the eternal man or woman. It's not an image of a particular man or woman; it is more general and universal than that. But it is this image that determines the sort of man or woman we are attracted to.

The *shadow* is more accessible to us than the anima and the animus. We can get a picture of it by looking into the personal unconscious. As we saw in the last chapter, such reflection is neither easy nor comfortable. Jung points out that the shadow "is a moral problem that challenges the whole ego-personality."[12] We naturally resist facing up to our dark side.

When we look at the "dark traits" that make up the shadow, we see that they have an emotional nature and, further, that they possess a high level of autonomy. Since we are not completely in control of these inferiorities, they tend to get control of us.

One very important reason for attempting to become conscious of the contents of the shadow side is that unless we do, we end up projecting our inferiorities. That is, we cast the failings that are our shadows onto others. This is an unconscious process. We don't say to ourselves, "I don't like having to deal with all my inferiorities; I think I'll get rid of some by dumping them on someone else." The unconscious operates according to its own laws, and it decides to project the shadow.

Up to this point, we have referred to the shadow in completely negative terms. It is important to be cognizant of the fact that as well as being an expression of evil impulses, it is also a source of dynamism and creativity. The shadow does in fact contain good qualities, normal instincts, and creative impulses. But of course it is the morally inferior qualities that are the difficult ones to acknowledge. If we try to ignore or deny these, the shadow will rise up against us. Bringing the contents of the shadow into consciousness is an important part of the movement toward wholeness.

The organizing principle in the personality is the archetype that Jung refers to as the *Self*. The role of the Self is to promote the reconciliation of opposites. The persona and the shadow are in opposition and they need to be able to find a way to exist together in a creative tension. Similarly, the male and female dimensions in the psyche need to be reconciled. In a word, the Self aims at psychic wholeness. When a person feels at peace with herself and with the world it is working very effectively.

In moving toward the state of self-realization it is necessary for the ego to cooperate. If the ego does not pick up on the messages from the Self, there is no possibility of understanding one's psyche. Self-realization can only occur when the ego is prepared to make conscious that which has been unconscious. The Self is an inner guiding force. We need to listen to it if we are to achieve individuation and wholeness.

In searching for a symbol of the completeness associated with the individuation process, Jung turns to Christ.[13] "He represents a totality of a divine or heavenly kind, a glorified man, a son of God *sine macula peccati,* unspotted by sin."[14] Since the Self represents the totality of personhood, both the conscious and the unconscious, it can only be symbolized through "antinomial" or oppositional terms. As we have just seen, there is within the psyche an oppositional relationship between the persona and the shadow, and between male and female aspects. In order to make the connection between the Self and Christ, Jung needs to find "antinomial terms" in the Christ symbol. He identifies two quaternions of opposites.[15] The first is comprised of the matched sets unitemporal-eternal and unique-universal. The Christ entered human history at a particular time in the person of Jesus of Nazareth and in him adopted a unique set of human characteristics. We can therefore refer to him through the terms "unitemporal" and "unique." But at the same time, Christ is divine and therefore eternal and universal.

To describe the other quaternion of opposites, Jung uses the following matched pairings: good-evil and spiritual-material. In Christ there is no evil, but the Christian tradition acknowledges the opposition of Satan. As Jung puts it: "[I]f theology describes Christ as simply 'good' and 'spiritual,' something 'evil' and 'material'—or 'chthonic'—is bound to arise on the other side, to represent the Antichrist."[16] This is so for Jung because inherent in human existence is a need for balance through opposition. Hot is defined by cold, high by low, and light by darkness; this is the nature of our world of experience.

In positing Christ as the symbol of the Self, Jung is aware of the possibility that some will want to turn things around. That is, there will be those who put the Self as the archetype of Christ. Here Jung makes reference to the famous *lapis philosophorum* or philosopher's stone. The *lapis* was for the medieval alchemists a symbol of perfection. Thus they naturally associated it with Christ. But the stone was elevated to a status it had no legitimate right to. In surveying the writings of the alchemists, Jung found "views and ideas which attach such importance to the stone that one begins to wonder whether, in the end, it was Christ who was taken as a symbol of the stone rather than the other way round."[17] Parallel to this inflation of the importance of the *lapis* is the human tendency to raise ourselves to the sphere of the divine. "Modern psychology is . . . confronted with a question very like the one that faced the alchemists: Is the self a symbol of Christ, or is Christ a symbol of the self?"[18]

Jung has already indicated how he resolves this issue. He also goes on to identify the problems associated with assigning the archetype of the Self the preeminent role. Anyone who reverses the real situation fails to recognize the considerable difference between perfection and completeness. Though Christ represents perfection through his sinlessness, it is not this fact that makes him a symbol of the Self. Sinlessness does not typify human selfhood. The Christ symbol typifies the Self because it contains the two quaternions of opposites. These quaternions capture the completeness that is the goal of self-realization. In the reversal, this proper relation between perfection and completeness is completely lost sight of: "The Christ-image is as good as perfect (at least it is meant to be so), while the archetype (so far as known) denotes completeness but is far from being perfect."[19] In a word, only in God do we find perfection.

But what happens when we take the archetype of the Self as the real agent in the process? That is, what is the practical outcome of positing the Self as the archetype of Christ? Jung suggests, first, that it is no bad thing to strive after perfection. In fact, the moral achievements of the European civilization are grounded in such a striving. There is, however, a very large shadow hanging over that civilization—one that is not sufficiently acknowledged when the archetype is assigned the active role. The crux of the matter for Jung is that we can freely choose individuation, or we can allow it to be forced on us.

If we one-sidedly concentrate on our moral achievements, the shadow will rise up and demand attention. The movement toward completeness is a struggle. To face one's inner opposites is no easy task. Indeed, it is like descending into "a deep pit." But we can freely take on the burden. It is better to walk into it with one's eyes open, says Jung, than to fall into it backwards. When there is a prideful elevation of the Self, the unconscious rises up in protest. Completeness is something forced upon one. That is, the shadow will not be denied; it will come at you, ready or not. Here Jung makes reference to the inner struggle as depicted by Paul in Romans 7: "The individual may strive after perfection . . . but must suffer from the opposite of his intentions for the sake of his completeness. 'I find then a law, when I would do good, evil is present within me.' "[20]

Jung here brings a psychological interpretation to Paul's theological analysis of the human condition. A central idea for Jung, as we have seen, is that the Self seeks to maintain balance. Thus, a psychic thrust too far in one direction will result in a push in the opposite direction. Jung contends that this psychological dynamic is driving the spiritual conflict described by Paul. A person driven by an ideal of perfect goodness will "stir up" the shadow. Feeling slighted, he will make his presence felt. The question arises: Does Paul advocate pursuit of moral perfection? I don't believe that he does. Indeed, the clear implication of his theology in Romans 7 is that it is folly to strive for perfect goodness. One should seek to advance in goodness, but the fact that the law of sin has such a strong hold means that moral perfection is simply not a possibility.

In another place, Paul teaches: "Do not conform yourselves to the standards of this world, but let God transform you inwardly by a complete change of your mind. Then you will be able to know the will of God—what is good and is pleasing to him and is perfect" (Rom 12:2). The divine will is perfection; we are not. We should be attempting to embrace God's will ever more fully, but Paul knows that we will never live it to perfection. The sinful self is like a squatter who has taken up residence in the soul. We may wish to evict him, but try as we might he simply will not budge. Once we catch hold of this, we free ourselves from a futile, and ultimately quite destructive, drive to perfection. It will be useful to explore these issues more fully.

PAUL AND THE INNER STRUGGLE

There has been considerable exegetical debate surrounding the "I" who makes confession in Romans 7: 14-25. Is it to be taken first and foremost as indicating Paul's personal experience? Or is it simply a literary device which is meant to refer to the "universal I," to the plight of each and every human? Some scholars have suggested that in the early verses the "I" who is speaking is the pious Jew, while in the latter verses it is the unredeemed person (E. Käsemann). Whomever we should take to be the "I" who is making confession, the salient fact for us is that Paul is obviously keenly aware that within himself—and we can assume that he did not think himself alone in this—there is a fundamental opposition. For the sake of simplicity, let us assume the "I" refers to Paul.

Käsemann[21] suggests that the key to understanding this inherent opposition within the self that is depicted by Paul is to be found in verse 14c: "I am a creature of flesh and blood sold as a slave to sin." This functions as a heading for the passage. Possessed by sin, it is inevitable that at every turn there will be a forced exchange of the good that is desired with the evil that is unwanted. It is not just that evil has an influence; Paul sees himself as "demonically enslaved."

In describing the battle he is in, Paul casts his "inmost self" against the "law of sin." That he regularly experiences defeat in his intention to live according to the divine will is the result of being a prisoner to this law: "In my inmost self I dearly love God's law, but I see that acting on my body there is a different law which battles against the law in my mind. So I am brought to be prisoner of that law of sin which lives inside my body" (vv. 22-23). Here, then, Paul recognizes very clearly that he is caught in the battle between his inner opposites. The inmost self represents the self that is oriented to God's will. Over against this self is the law of sin. "Law" here is meant in the sense of a principle or rule of action.[22] Or it can also be understood as a "squatter."[23] He is not legitimately in residence, but he is very difficult to evict. He is also a very powerful squatter, because he takes Paul prisoner and directs him against his better intentions. Paul's perception of the real situation within the human self shows up most vividly the folly of moral perfectionism. Leon Morris puts it this way in his commentary on the passage: "Every earnest Christian advances in goodness, but cannot arrive at perfection. Why not? Because he is sold under sin."[24]

With this vulnerability to sin in mind, Suzanne Mayer suggests that we should subscribe to the motto that her friend John Sanford was so fond of: "Perfect and still improving."[25] His ironic comment reminds us that it is misguided to believe that we can ever completely vanquish the shadow. With this in mind, Jung teaches that wholeness rather than perfection is the appropriate goal. Moral perfectionism results in unnecessary feelings of failure, guilt, and worthlessness. Jung suggests that what we should be aiming for instead is progress on the journey into completeness. We move toward completeness through a reconciliation of psychic opposites.

RECONCILIATION OF INNER OPPOSITES

The first task in moving toward a reconciliation of the opposites within is to recognize and acknowledge what is really there. Up to this point, we have cast the shadow in completely negative terms. It is important to recognize, as was mentioned above, that as well as being an expression of evil impulses, it is also a source of dynamism and creativity. "[T]he unconscious man, that is, his shadow," writes Jung, "does not consist only of morally reprehensible tendencies, but also displays a number of good qualities, such as normal instincts, appropriate reactions, realistic insights, creative impulses, etc."[26] But of course it is the "morally reprehensible" qualities that are the difficult ones to acknowledge. If we try to ignore or deny these, the shadow will rise up against us.

More than insight, it takes courage to acknowledge the shadow. Looking the negative self squarely in the face always results in an assault on self-esteem. It is for this reason that we tend to gloss over the differences we have with the dark side. However, there can never be any progress toward reconciliation when we settle for an easy accommodation. What is required is an honest dialogue with the shadow. This dialogue centers on this fundamental question: "What are we going to do to enable us to constructively live together?" It is not only a question of what the shadow will do in changing for the better, although this is certainly an important part of the process. It is also a matter of what I will offer the shadow. He may need to hear "the truth spoken in love"; but he will also need acceptance, love, and patience. Reconciliation or enmity with the shadow is in our hands. M.-L. von Franz puts it this way:

> Whether the shadow becomes our friend or enemy depends largely upon ourselves . . . [T]he shadow is not necessarily always an opponent. In fact, he is exactly like any human being with whom one has to get along, sometimes by giving in, sometimes by resisting, sometimes by giving love—whatever the situation requires. The shadow becomes hostile only when he is ignored or misunderstood.[27]

von Franz indicates that the destructive side of the shadow must be resisted for the sake of growth and well-being. Even as we resist, though, there needs to be love and understanding. Nothing is to be gained by condemning the shadow; hostility rather than reconciliation will be the outcome.[28]

von Franz's suggestion that we should sometimes simply give in to the shadow calls for comment. Jung expresses the relationship with the shadow differently. His emphasis is not on acquiescing to it, but rather on seeking to correct it:

> Everyone carries a shadow, and the less it is embodied in the individual's conscious life, the blacker and denser it is. If an inferiority is conscious, one always has a chance to correct it. Furthermore, it is constantly in contact with other interests, so that it is continually subjected to modifications. But if it is repressed and isolated from consciousness, it never gets corrected.[29]

This approach fits much better with gospel values. Given that Christians are called to aim for conformity to Christ, it should not be our intent to accede to morally inferior impulses. Sometimes, of course, we do in fact give in. This is Paul's point: "I find then a law, when I would do good, evil is present within me." Our aim is always to align ourselves more closely with the way of Christ; sometimes we miss the mark. From a Christian perspective, reconciliation with the shadow involves recognition, honesty, understanding, and acceptance. The idea that part of the process is to sometimes choose to give in to the shadow seems contrary to the gospel ethic.

There is another dimension in the message of Romans 7 that is very important in the context of our discussion. Jung says time and again in his writings that he concentrates only on the psychological dynamics associated with religious doctrines. As a psychologist, it would be inappropriate for him to engage in theological reflection. Jung is quite right to take this position. However, as a theologian I need to point out that the story does not begin and end for Paul with the battle between his inner opposites. While he recognizes that inner conflict will always be with us in this lifetime ("What a wretched man I am" [v. 24]), he also holds onto the eschatological hope for the wholeness that Christ offers us ("Thanks be to God—through Jesus Christ our Lord!" [v. 25]).

COMPLETENESS IN CHRIST

As we have seen, the Romans 7 passage is essentially an elaboration of the theme "sold under sin." The inmost self aims to shape a life faithful to God's calling, but it is held prisoner by the law of sin. This law subverts all of our moral and spiritual processes, including individuation, from time to time. We find ourselves knocking our heads against a wall that blocks our progress. Sometimes it seems like we have smashed through, only to find another wall confronting us. There are times when we feel a relative inner peace. But on other occasions we become acutely aware of the power of the squatter within. It is then that we resonate with Paul's cry: "How wretched I am."

Our deepest hope is not to be found in our capacity to recognize the shadow and work with him in growing into our uniqueness as persons. The hope of individuation is an important one, but it is only provisional. Completeness is an eschatological reality. Our eternal destiny is perfect wholeness in God. Ernst Käsemann sums up Paul's hope, and ours, with these eloquent words: "When [the human] comes to an end of himself, creation out of nothing can follow, the pneuma can clothe the shadow with new corporeality and the possessed of the world can become the eschatological [freedpersons] of God."[30]

SUMMARY

Moral perfectionism is extremely detrimental to our psychological and spiritual health. It is a good thing to aim for moral improvement, but to compulsively strive for impossibly high standards results in feelings of failure, guilt, and worthlessness. Jung's suggestion that we should seek after completeness rather than perfection is helpful. Completeness is the goal of the process of individuation or self-realization. It involves a reconciliation of inner opposites. Christ is the archetype of this reconciliation process and therefore of the Self. If we attempt to reverse the situation and establish the Self as the symbol of Christ, we find that completeness is forced on us. That is, in the hubris of inflating ourselves to divine proportions, the shadow is ignored. But the shadow will not be denied; it will rise up and make its presence felt. Far better, says Jung, to freely take on the burden of individuation.

For his part, Paul acknowledges fully the place of the shadow. In Romans 7 he recognizes both the inmost self that is oriented to God's will and the law of sin that pulls us away from that will. Moreover, the shadow will always be with us. The clear implication is that aiming for perfect goodness is futile, and ultimately destructive. Importantly, Paul also reminds us that our hope for completeness is eschatological. In rising with Christ, the conflicts, distortions, and ambiguities within the psyche will finally be resolved.

Chapter 4

Cognitive Reframing and Perfectionism

In the previous chapter, we reflected on the pain that is associated with a compulsive striving after impossibly high standards of goodness and love. That is, we were concerned about the plague of perfectionism. It is important to recognize that this is a particular kind of perfectionism, namely, one that is grounded in guilt. Judging that we have fallen short of the moral mark, we are assailed by guilty feelings. The superego has gone into overdrive and we pay for it with feelings of failure and unworthiness. Along with guilt-based perfectionism, however, there is a shame-based form. Whereas guilt is associated with moral transgression, shame is connected with feelings of inferiority and inadequacy. The focus of a perfectionism grounded in guilt is moral failure. When it comes to shame-based perfectionism, the feelings of inadequacy are associated with a sense of falling short of a cherished ideal. That is, one feels that one has been tested and has been found wanting. Often the shame is connected to failure in a task or project. Of course, we all have this experience from time to time. Perfectionism enters the picture when the sense of failure stems from a tendency to establish unrealistic expectations for personal achievement and to strain compulsively to meet those expectations.

I want to suggest that shame-based perfectionism can be traced to a faulty core belief about the self, and that is: "I am what I achieve." This core belief is fundamentally flawed because it can never deliver what we really need. What is ultimately most important is a personal conviction, affirmed by significant others and by God, that one is

Moving Toward Spiritual Maturity
© 2007 by The Haworth Press, Inc. All rights reserved.
doi:10.1300/5886_04

good, worthy, and lovable. This conviction refers to personhood and not to achievement. Others will *respect* and *admire* our achievements; they will *love* and *value* the persons that we are. Achievement can never deliver what we most value.

The idea of a core belief comes from the school of cognitive therapy. Put simply, this school believes that emotional distress flows from distorted thinking. If we can learn to think more realistically, our mental health will be enhanced. Aaron Beck and his associates have developed a particular approach built around three levels of thinking: automatic thoughts, intermediate beliefs, and core beliefs. I will attempt to show how shame-based perfectionism can be dealt with at the two upper levels. The thought worksheets that cognitive therapists work with are valuable self-help aids, and I will demonstrate their use.

GUILT-BASED AND SHAME-BASED PERFECTIONISM

Those of us who have been involved in the life of the church over many years are no strangers to the concept of guilt. It fills the pages of our Bibles and of our hymnbooks. The message of sin, guilt, and the forgiveness Christ has won for us has been featured in countless sermons. It is a message that is elevated and celebrated every year in the Easter festival. We understand very well what guilt is.

Shame sits in a different category, though. Although it is true that the experience of feeling ashamed is not foreign to us, it is also the case that we tend not to understand shame nearly as well as we do guilt. Shame is fundamentally about feeling unworthy, inferior, inadequate, or flawed in some way. An early experience of shame for me has as its context my regular holiday visits to the city when I was in upper primary school. We lived in outback Australia and every year my parents would take us to the Gold Coast for a beach holiday. Before moving on to our final destination, we would spend a few days catching up with our relatives in Brisbane, the capital city of our state. At that time I would renew my acquaintance with my cousin, Hugh. I always thought of Hugh as being a really cool kid. He wore the latest gear—cool T-shirt and Levi's jeans. He was into all the latest pop music. And he knew all the "in" language. Hugh seemed to feel that his mission in life was to bring his poor country cousin into the world of "cool." I was a willing pupil, but I never really felt like I was making the grade. I thought of Hugh as living an elevated existence. I saw him as living on a plane that I could reach up for, but would never fully attain.

Shame is the major cause of emotional distress in the Western world today, according to some psychologists.[1] It is all around us. Some of us may think that this is an exaggeration. Perhaps one reason for thinking that this is the case is that shame-prone people can be quite good at hiding their feelings of inferiority and inadequacy. There are actually quite a few more shame-sufferers out there than one might think; it is sometimes difficult to penetrate into their defensive walls. This fact was brought home for me when I read an article in a pastoral care journal that was written by a colleague of mine. Richard has always presented to me as highly intelligent, witty, urbane, and self-confident. He would be the last person that I would expect to be plagued by shame feelings. When I read his article titled "Confessing Dying Within," however, I learned something very important about him. The last section of the article he calls "Concluding by Example," and in it he makes what for me was quite a revelation:

> Two years ago, for two short periods separated by twelve months, I assisted, as a home hospice care volunteer, a person who was suffering from AIDS, who died during the last period of my care. After farewelling him and awaiting the end, I returned home, and woke up in the middle of the night in a state well described by various words used by [shame theorists], such as "empty, exhausted, drained, demoralized, depressed, deflated, bereft, needy, starving, apathetic, passive and weak." I cried inconsolably over his tragic loss, as I thought about him. One of my fellow workers, from whom I sought comfort, suggested that I get further help. I remain grateful to her. I now know that my grief was over my depleted self, of which Ken's physical depletion was but a mirror. The point of this glimpse of autobiography is that confession as I had known it was no path to healing . . . [Healing came through] a welcome to both parts of my separated self, the self that had successfully done many useful things, and continued to do so, and the self who for almost as long as I could remember continually told me, "You are shit."[2]

Shame is everywhere to be seen, but still it remains something of a mystery to many of us. We are much more familiar with guilt, and we tend to simply lump shame and guilt together. Indeed, it is the case that guilt and shame cannot be easily distinguished. This is because they share a good deal of overlap; they are cousins in the family of affects, if you will. Both involve a negative judgment on the self and both adversely affect mood. Further, because guilt and shame are often bound up together they are difficult to dissociate in personal experience.

Guilt is commonly distinguished from shame through a reference to the global scope of the latter. Guilt can be localized, but shame affects the whole person. That is, though I *do* bad things that cause me to feel guilty, I *am* my shame. I feel guilty when I have morally transgressed, and what I need in order to feel better is forgiveness. I have experienced a temporary drop in my self-esteem due to the feeling that I have acted badly. For the person prone to shame, however, low self-esteem is an ongoing and pervasive problem. This is so because *I* am the problem. I feel inferior, inadequate, and virtually worthless. My need is not for forgiveness but rather for love, affirmation, and acceptance. Helen Block Lewis brings out these distinctions very clearly when she compares the self-reproaches in guilty thinking with those of ashamed thinking:

> [Guilt-laden cognitions run thus:] "How could I have *done that,* what an injurious *thing* to have done; how I *hurt so-and-so,* what a moral lapse that *act* was; what will become of *that* or of *him,* now that I have neglected to *do it,* or injured *him.* How should I be *punished* or *make amends?* Mea culpa!" Simultaneously, ashamed ideation says: "how could *I* have done that; what an *idiot I am*—how humiliating; what a *fool,* what an *uncontrolled person*—how mortifying; how unlike so-and-so, who does not do such things; how *awful and worthless I am.* Shame!"[3] (emphasis in the original)

With this information before us, it is quite easy to describe a guilt-based perfectionism. Those of us who suffer from this affliction are constantly setting our goals for good and right living at an unrealistically high level. We are acutely aware of the fact that Christ calls us to a life of love, goodness, and justice. If we could be content with improvement in striving after the ideal, all would be well. But our problem is that we need perfection. No matter what level of conformity to Christ we reach, it is never good enough. We show compassion to others when they fail, but sadly we hold it back from ourselves.

In order to describe shame-based perfectionism, we need to make some distinctions in relation to the phenomenon of shame. This is a very diverse phenomenon. As theologian Stephen Pattison observes in his comprehensive study on approaches to shame, there is "no constant essence or basis to shame," but rather a "family resemblance."[4] The family, moreover, is not especially close-knit. Here are some of its members. There is the "situational"[5] shame we experience when we embarrass ourselves in public. For instance, in giving a speech we suffer through an unfortunate slip of the tongue. People also feel shame over their inherited identity. To be a member of a certain family—"He's one of those Smiths"—or of a certain ethnic grouping can cause shame for some. There is also shame that is related to physical appearance. A person may be very talented, but shamed by his or her obesity. Or a handsome person who once knew only pride in his or her appearance experiences deep shame after a disfiguring car accident.

The two members of the shame family that are most commonly referred to are *moral* shame and *inferiority* shame. In the case of the first type, guilt and shame are tangled up together. When there has been a moral failure we feel a burden of guilt, but we also feel shame. So even though I have made reference to guilt-based perfectionism, it is evident that shame will be part of this experience as well. I have used this label because guilt is the dominant or primary affect involved. Inferiority shame, on the other hand, is connected with the need to achieve and to be successful. It refers to a propensity for feeling inadequate and incompetent in relation to the major tasks required by one's plan of life.

Shame-based perfectionism is associated with inferiority shame. The construction of the self as developed by Heinz Kohut that we discussed in Chapter 2 is helpful in understanding this form of shame. Recall that Kohut posits a bipolar self: a grandiose self and an idealizing self. The first is shaped around talents and achievements, the second around goals and ambitions. Shame results when the idealizing self, making the judgment that the grandiose self has failed, goes on the attack: "You're no good; you're a disgrace. I had such high hopes and you have failed miserably."

We are confronted with our limitations quite early in life. It is when we begin school that we become especially aware of the areas in which we are inferior, as Erik Erikson has pointed out. Erikson is famous for his description of the eight stages of human development.[6] Each stage, or "crisis," is described in bipolar terms: trust versus mistrust, autonomy versus shame and doubt, initiative versus guilt, and so on. The school-age crisis is defined in terms of industry versus inferiority. A school student develops a sense of industry when she judges that she is able to perform the tasks set before her competently. Conversely, when she experiences herself as failing in her educational assignments she feels inferior.

Erikson points to the fact that a tendency in some men (and today, of course, we would include a growing number of women in this) to define identity in terms of work and achievements has its origin in a certain form of education. An educational philosophy with little or no appreciation for the importance of the development of the whole person will contribute to a sense of identity shaped around the thought "I am what I can learn to make work."[7]

Whereas guilt-based perfectionism is associated with moral improvement, shame-based perfectionism is task-oriented and focused on achievement. In all the various tasks of life there is scope for setting impossibly high standards. Perfectionism should, however, be distinguished from striving for excellence.[8] Working diligently on the projects that we have chosen for ourselves is appropriate and it is not incompatible with good mental health. We do need to check, however, whether or not we can still feel satisfied with our efforts despite some slipups. If this is the case, we are being realistic. The perfectionist never feels satisfied because she or he is striving for impossibly high levels of achievement. Driven to achieve at higher and higher levels, the results are never considered to be good enough.

I suggest that behind shame-based perfectionism is the core belief "I am what I achieve." The notion of core beliefs comes from cognitive therapy. In this form of therapy, the aim is to reshape distorted patterns of thinking. The dysfunctional core belief associated with perfectionism can be replaced over time with a more realistic and healthy one. I want to first describe the core concepts and interventions in cognitive therapy. This information will then be used to indicate a strategy for dealing with perfectionism.

THE BASICS OF COGNITIVE THERAPY

Aaron Beck and his associates are part of the school of psychotherapy known as cognitive therapy and they subscribe to its basic premise, namely that a person's emotions and behaviors are primarily shaped by her cognitions. A person thinks negatively and the results are dysfunctional feelings and behaviors. Beck and his co-workers have listed common cognitive distortions that lead to dysphoria[9] (my illustrations):

1. *All-or-nothing thinking.* Viewing a situation at its extremes rather than along a continuum: "If I'm not perfect in my parenting, I'm a bad mom/dad."
2. *Catastrophizing.* You tend to always see disaster: "I've been messing up at work lately; I'm on a downward spiral."
3. *Discounting the positive.* You find ways to discredit your successes: "Yeah okay, I'm good at home maintenance jobs, but all that takes is a bit of common sense."
4. *Emotional reasoning.* You think something must be true because you "feel" it strongly: "Others seem to rate me as competent in my job, but I still feel like I'm not making the grade."
5. *Labeling.* You define yourself through a negative category, discounting evidence to the contrary: "I'm a failure."
6. *Magnifying the negative and minimizing the positive.* When you evaluate yourself or a situation, you magnify the negative and/or minimize the positive: "Okay, it might be only one low grade, but it proves that I'm not really much good after all." Or, "I expected a good mark from her; she's a soft assessor."
7. *Mind reading.* You believe that you know what others are thinking: "My boss wasn't very friendly during the coffee break this morning. That confirms my suspicions that she isn't happy with my work."
8. *Overgeneralization.* You make a sweeping negative judgment based on one bad experience: "I was tense and muffed a few of

the lines in my talk; I don't have what it takes to be good at public speaking."

9. *Personalization.* You attribute the negative behavior of others to a personal lack or failing: A friend is sounding a little emotionally flat on the telephone, and you assume it's because he's disappointed with you.

10. *"Should" and "must" statements.* You have a rigid understanding of how you should think and act: "I must always be nice in my relations with others, no matter what."

Beck started with the notion of automatic thoughts that run through our heads—such as the ones just listed—but later expanded his understanding of the cognitive model to include intermediate beliefs and core beliefs. The thoughts that flash through a person's mind in any given situation, shaping her feelings and her actions, flow from core and intermediate beliefs. Beck's daughter, Judith, defines the three components in the cognitive model in this way:

> *Core beliefs* are the most fundamental level of belief; they are global, rigid, and overgeneralized. *Automatic thoughts,* the actual words or images that go through a person's mind, are situation specific and may be considered the most superficial level of cognition. . . . Core beliefs influence the development of an intermediate class of beliefs which consist of (often unarticulated) attitudes, rules, and assumptions.[10]

The relationship between the three dimensions in the cognitive process may be illustrated with reference to a person who has a propensity for shame. He attempts to compensate for his inferiority feelings by entertaining others. His humor is often inappropriate and not particularly funny. The *core belief* that he operates out of is, "I'm inferior." At the intermediate level, there is the *attitude,* "Other people tend not to like me"; the *rule,* "I must use humor to impress others"; and the *assumption,* "Humor is necessary if I'm to keep the attention of others." With these beliefs operating, when he finds himself in a situation of making a new acquaintance, the *automatic thought* flashes through his head, "She probably won't like me but my only chance is to impress her with my wit."

In general terms, the cognitive therapist begins by focusing on automatic thoughts. These are the cognitions closest to conscious awareness. The client is trained to identify, evaluate, and modify these thoughts in order to gain relief from her symptoms. Once this area of treatment has been consolidated, the underlying beliefs are targeted. The modification of intermediate and core beliefs leads to a fundamental change in the way a person interprets particular situations and events. A change in perceptual outlook leads to a more positive emotional reaction.

The cognitive therapist trains the client to identify and evaluate the automatic thoughts that are leading to depression and anxiety. Once he knows what automatic thoughts are associated with his problems, the therapist works with him on challenging these dysfunctional cognitions. He is trained to ask himself

1. about the evidence for and against the idea,
2. whether there is an alternative explanation,
3. what the worst outcome might be (and whether he thinks he can cope with it),
4. what the impact of believing the automatic thought is, and
5. what the effect would be of changing his thinking.[11]

Once a client has identified an automatic thought and questioned it in this way, she can reshape it. What she is seeking to do is to replace the distorted cognition with a more realistic one. For example, Jane gets very anxious while meeting new people. She has been helped to identify the strongest, most insistent automatic thought associated with this fear: "This person probably won't like me." The counselor and Jane work together to form a more adaptive response: "I have a number of admirable qualities; most people will like me. In fact, that has been my experience in the past."

It is worth noting that the approach of the cognitive therapists can be integrated with core gospel principles and values. A basic affinity between the Christian religio-ethical system and cognitive therapy, as Stanton Jones has observed,[12] is that there is a common valuing of rationality and of right thinking. Cognitive therapy grounds itself in the ability of the human to rationally analyze her thought processes and belief systems. The Christian faith also emphasizes the importance of thinking rightly, of orienting our minds to God and to God's teaching. In the collection of wise thoughts, that is, the book of Proverbs, we read: "As a person thinks in his heart, so he is" (23:7).

In cognitive therapy there is an optimistic view that bad mental habits can be discarded and replaced by healthier ones. In the Bible we find a similarly optimistic view of the human potential for a positive construction of the mind. Paul talks about renewing the mind so that it conforms more closely to the mind of Christ (Rom 12:2). The implication is that the disciples of Christ are able to learn his core principles and values and apply them in the various circumstances they find themselves in. In a word, Christianity values rationality.

There is also a general affinity between the Christian tradition and cognitive therapy in relation to self-acceptance. As we have seen, a common irrational tendency identified by cognitive therapists is that of making negative judgments concerning the worth of the self as a global entity. It is legitimate for a person to evaluate some of her actions negatively, but a leap from judgments about isolated actions to a condemnation of the self as a whole is unwarranted. In a Christian understanding, we are called upon to critically evaluate our actions and seek God's forgiveness when we judge that we have morally transgressed. A judgment that one has sinned will always result in a temporary drop in self-esteem. But the knowledge that God accepts us unconditionally, that God loves us with all our imperfections and failings, serves as a powerful reminder that a pattern of self-condemnation is contrary to God's intention. The fact that God loves us and accepts us in spite of our frailty gives us every reason to love and accept ourselves. Alan Jones expresses this truth most eloquently. He refers to the confirming presence of the Holy Spirit:

> You may be neurotic; you may be mean; you may be miserly; you may be a whole kettle of horrors, but the most real thing about you is the Holy Spirit because you are the dwelling place of God. You are the temple of the Holy Spirit. That means that we do not have to be diminished by other people's definitions of us, or worse, our own definition of ourselves as unworthy or as ugly or as unacceptable. At our very deepest, there is the Spirit of God calling us.[13]

As well as noting these areas of affinity, it is important for our purposes to note that the basic principles of cognitive therapy can be readily applied outside of therapy.[14] This form of counseling is particularly suited to self-help. A core tool provided by the cognitive therapists is the belief worksheet. It gives us a framework for purposively working through our cognitive distortions and for establishing more constructive patterns of thinking. Analyzing our distorted thinking lays the foundation for assembling evidence that supports a more realistic and healthy cognitive approach. I will demonstrate how these worksheets can be employed in mitigating perfectionism.

DEALING WITH SHAME-BASED PERFECTIONISM

Consider the following scenario.

Wayne is a lay leader in his congregation and chairs his church council. It is the morning after a particularly difficult meeting of the council and he is reflecting on how he handled it. In his three years in the leadership role, Wayne has been attempting to deal with two strong leaders who exercise a disproportionate influence on the Council. At the previous night's meeting he was feeling tired and was not as sharp as he usually is. His interventions from the chair were not especially well timed. Moreover, they were wide off the mark and consequently ineffective in restraining the power brokers, and the meeting moved with them in a direction that Wayne felt was unhelpful. On the morning after he is kicking himself. He realizes that he let the meeting get away from him and he feels like a total failure.

Wayne is prone to shame. Though he is a competent person, he is plagued by feelings of inferiority and inadequacy. Wayne works extremely hard and sets very high standards for himself. He tells himself that Christ calls us to service and deserves our very best. His cover story is that he is striving for excellence in all that he does, and especially in his ministry of leadership. If you asked him about his tendency to depression, he would say something like this: "Of course I get disappointed with myself sometimes. I set the bar high and when I don't quite make it I feel a bit down. That's natural, isn't it?" What is really going on, though, is that Wayne suffers from perfectionism. He needs his achievements in life to boost his self-esteem and self-confidence. But when he reaches a particular goal that he has set for himself he is disappointed with what is only a slight and temporary improvement in his self-esteem. Consequently, he needs to keep lifting the bar higher. His pattern is to push harder and harder in order to feel better about himself. Tragically, he is tying his self-worth to a disproportionate degree to his level of skill and effectiveness in the tasks he performs.

Wayne is trapped in this destructive pattern. Sadly, the only story that is available to him is the one that tells him that if only he can lift his level of achievement will he find the inner peace and positive self-esteem that have so far eluded him. Imagine, though, that Wayne picks up a copy of David Burns' book, *Feeling Good*. There he discovers how the principles of cognitive therapy can be applied in one's everyday life. His eyes are opened. He begins to see that there is another way, a much better way, of thinking about how he operates in the world. Wayne decides to read some more books on cognitive therapy. Finally, he makes a decision to use the belief modification worksheets that he has been reading about. The cognitive reframing that he engages in operates at the level of both intermediate and core belief. His worksheets are set out in Figures 4.1 and 4.2.

Through his reflections, Wayne discovers that operating at a level higher than the belief "I am a failure as a leader" is the core belief "I am what I achieve." He realizes that he is striving for perfection in a misguided attempt to boost his sense of self-worth. A deep realization dawns that what he really needs is an inner conviction that he is right, good, and full of quality. Wayne is aware that this affirmation

Situation	Attitudes, rules, and assumptions	The intermediate belief	Adaptive response	Reframed intermediate belief
I wasn't able to effectively manage the church council meeting a few weeks ago. My interventions were ill timed and wide of the mark.	*Attitude:* I messed up; I really don't have what it takes to be a leader. *Rules:* Each and every time I lead a meeting I must operate at maximum competency. *Assumption:* The fact that I didn't handle the meeting very well means that I'm a failure.	I'm a failure as a leader.	*Cognitive Distortions:* Overgeneralization. One lapse indicates total failure in leadership. All-or-nothing thinking. I am either a complete success or a complete failure. *Realistic responses:* One lapse does not make me a failure. To have an off night now and then is to be human. Feedback from others indicates that I have good leadership skills.	I am an effective leader who sometimes makes mistakes.

FIGURE 4.1. Wayne's Intermediate Belief Worksheet.

can only come through *relationship*. He knows that he can look to friends and family for confirmation of his value as a person. But he also reaffirms his need to look to God's love and acceptance in Christ for affirmation. He is led to the liberating insight that there is a kind of uselessness about human life.[15] A person is useless in the sense that God affirms him or her as full of worth and quality quite apart from anything he or she may achieve.

Through using these worksheets, Wayne is able, over time, to reframe his intermediate and core beliefs. As his core cognitions become healthier, more realistic, his perfectionism is mitigated. But, of course, it is an ongoing struggle; progress toward the goal of living in a more wholesome way is hard won. Suzanne Mayer uses the telling expression "recovering perfectionists."

Old core belief: I am what I achieve.
How much do I believe the old core belief at the moment? 80 percent
New belief: Before any achievement I am worthy.
How much do I believe the new belief at the moment? 40 percent

Evidence that contradicts old core belief and supports new belief	Evidence that supports new belief
I work harder and harder; I achieve certain goals that seemed so significant; and yet I still feel unworthy. I never feel satisfied with myself. I perform my tasks well, but I know that I could have done better. "Good" is not good enough for me. When I am pushing myself I tell myself that I will celebrate when the task is finished. But after all the effort, I'm not as happy as I thought I would be. It seems like I'm looking in the wrong place.	Sometimes when I am alone with God I feel God's love and I'm happy to be me. I know that when it's all said and done, the relationships I have with my wife and kids are what really count. What I really want most is simply to know that I am loved and accepted by God and by those closest to me. The story of the Prodigal. Boy, he failed in spectacular fashion! What did the father do? He ran to embrace him and celebrated his homecoming. Really, the father celebrated the son. It wasn't a celebration of achievements—there weren't any— but simply a celebration of a person and of a relationship.

FIGURE 4.2. Wayne's Core Belief Worksheet.

[L]ike the alcoholic—who, once aware of his or her problem, can maintain sobriety only by admitting that he or she is never recovered but always working on it—the past perfectionist is one who constantly feels pulled to slip back into the demanding, overly conscientious way of thinking and behavior that makes life miserable but so well done.[16]

The recovering perfectionist needs to stick at the task of reframing his or her core cognitions to avoid the pull back into destructive patterns.

SUMMARY

Shame-based perfectionism involves a compulsive striving after impossibly high standards of achievement. I have argued that behind it is the core belief "I am what I achieve." But success, though it can be pleasant and satisfying, can never deliver what the shame-prone person really needs, namely love and acceptance. This can only come through relationships. It is in relation with God and with others that we are affirmed in our personhood. With this in mind, I have suggested that the core belief the perfectionist needs to embrace is this: "Before any achievement I am worthy."

PART III:
PRAYER, CONTEMPLATION, AND CONVERSION

Chapter 5

Spirituality in the Everyday World

In this section of our reflections, the idea of finding God in the stuff of everyday life will crop up time and again. The major theme is conversion to the way of Christ. However, I will be attempting to show that a very important arena for transformation in Christ is that of the ordinary that we are immersed in for so much of our lives. Though I do not agree with all aspects of Thomas Moore's approach to spirituality, he captures the mood behind my approach perfectly when he writes: "Only when ordinary life and deep spirituality come together do we find our humanity, our community and interdependency, a basis for morality, and our saving compassion."[1]

In the older approach to spirituality, the world was viewed negatively. It was the locus of distractions and temptations. All the business of life was seen, first, as pulling a person away from a deep life of prayer and communion with God. To be in the world is to be distracted from the highest calling in life, namely prayer and contemplation. Further, in the world there are all kinds of temptations to sin. In the world, one is confronted with the lure of sensual and material pleasures. Purity of heart can only be assured if one removes oneself from these sources of temptation.

In her book *Earth Crammed with Heaven*, Elizabeth Dreyer rightly observes that there has been a strong movement away from this kind of thinking.[2] The first step was to acknowledge that since our faith is built around the experience of an incarnate God, a God who has dwelt in the world, the world should not be cast in such a strongly negative light. Sin and evil are the enemies, not the world. But then there was a further step—one that constitutes a complete reversal of the old

Moving Toward Spiritual Maturity
© 2007 by The Haworth Press, Inc. All rights reserved.
doi:10.1300/5886_05

thinking. Contrary to viewing the world as a place of impurity and contamination, as an arena separated from grace, it is now seen as the primary place in which most people encounter God. To separate the sacred and the profane is to severely limit one's experience of the divine. Dreyer quotes the Hasidic saying: "Whoever says that the words of the Torah are one thing and the words of the world another must be regarded as a person who denies God." It is worth noting, however, that there have been those who have lived the way of separation from the world in order to concentrate on prayer and contemplation, and who have at the same time managed to stay vitally connected to the everyday world. The Trappist monk, Thomas Merton, vividly describes this experience when he writes:

> [T]hough "out of the world" we [monks] are in the same world as everybody else, the world of the bomb, the world of race hatred, the world of technology, the world of mass media, big business, revolution, and all the rest. We take a different attitude to all these things, for we belong to God. Yet so does everybody else belong to God . . . This sense of liberation from an illusory difference was such a relief and such a joy to me that I almost laughed out loud . . . And I suppose my happiness could have taken form in these words: "Thank God, thank God that I *am* like other men, that I am only a man among others."[3] (emphasis in the original)

It would be wrong, then, to dismiss any attempt to separate from the everyday world as outmoded and out of touch. Clearly, there are those who are "out of the world," but who remain very much connected with it. But what I want to concentrate on here is a spirituality of everyday life. In seeking to connect the spiritual life with the world of the everyday, there is a wide range of issues one could select for attention. One could, for example, attend to such important and omnipresent concerns as work and business, the experience of commuting, sleep, leisure activities and hobbies, television and cinema, the performing and the visual arts, and sport. But I have chosen to focus on these five central areas: *nature, the city, time, marriage and family,* and *sociopolitical systems and structures.* The fact that so many important areas have been left out should not cause us consternation. What I am aiming at in this limited discussion is simply to highlight the way in which we experience God in the world of the everyday. In addressing these five important dimensions, I will at least be able to draw a sketch of spirituality of life in the everyday world.

SPIRITUALITY AND NATURE

Many of us love to escape to the natural environment because it ministers to our souls. It "exhales a spirituality that can be healing and restoring and can mediate our need for the sublime and for divinity itself."[4] Out in the woods, or walking on the beach, or ascending to the mountaintop, we are able to breathe out the stale, heavy air of a city life characterized by artificiality and a certain madness and draw in the calming, restorative energy of the natural world.

The natural environment also provides a contemplative space. In the quiet and stillness of the woods, we can listen more attentively to God's voice. Caught in the busyness of the daily round, communion with God seems to get slotted in, or squeezed in, among all the other activities. In fact, it is often not really communion with God at all. Harassed and tired, we rush through the motions of prayer. But walking in the open air, the demands and pressures of life seem far away. They may be at least far away enough to find a space for listening to, for waiting on, the God we love and serve. In his book *Working the Angles,* Eugene Peterson tells of his practice of taking each Monday to go hiking into the hills with his wife. After a psalm and a prayer, they keep silence. When they have reached their destination, they share their reflective experiences:

> When the sun or our stomachs tell us it is lunchtime, we break the silence with a prayer of blessing for the sandwiches and the fruit, the river and the forest. We are free to talk now, sharing bird sightings, thoughts, observations, ideas—however much or little we are inclined.[5]

The natural world seems naturally to create a space for communion with God and with others.

Those who find nature a healing, restorative space are deeply aware of the connectedness of everything in the cosmos. "We are animal, our spirits interwoven with nature in a union so tight," reflects

Jeanette Batz, "we've managed to ignore it for centuries."[6] It's not only the fact that we're bound so closely to nature that stops modern Westerners from fully appreciating our intimate bond with the natural world. I suggest that what really obscures the fact of our communal relationship with nature is the fact that we are immersed in a Cartesian way of viewing reality. In the perspective of René Descartes (1596-1650), the world is construed in mechanistic and inanimate terms, and the human person is constructed as a detached, objective ego. The body and the mind are split apart, and human beings are separated from the machine-like world that they inhabit. The power of science in this paradigm resides in the fact that it can unlock the secrets of the "world machine" and use them in shaping, controlling, subduing, and exploiting it.

There is another model of the world that is available to us, however. In this paradigm, spirituality rather than science and technology is the animating source. In my own Australian culture, one can look to the worldview of the Aborigines as a source for this spirituality. The indigenous Australians feel intimately connected to the natural environment. They experience the Land as their mother. They have a deep respect for the Land, and their aim is always to live in harmony with it. There is no thought of gaining dominion over it or of exploiting it. Such thinking is an abomination to indigenous Australians. I remember going on a retreat in the Coorong district of South Australia. The retreat center that we stayed in was run by the tribe indigenous to the area. A representative of the tribe took us on a guided tour of the surrounds on the Saturday afternoon. He stopped at one point and said to the group:

> Look around you. Do you notice that the land here is virtually untouched. We had a government fella come out to us once. He said to us, "You blokes have had this land for a long time now. It's about time you did something with it. If you can't develop it a bit, we'll have to take it over from you." What I said to him was, "You don't get it, do you? This is just the way we like it. This is how it's supposed to be."

The approach to the land that Native Americans have is very similar to that of the Australian aborigines. Chief Luther Standing Bear observes:

Life for the Indian is one of harmony with Nature and the things which surround him. The Indian tried to fit in with Nature and to understand, not to conquer and to rule. We were rewarded by learning much that the white man will never know. Life was a glorious thing, for great contentment comes with the feeling of friendship and kinship with the living things around you.[7]

This kinship or communion with the natural world is also reflected in the spirituality of Francis of Assisi. In his famous canticle, he declares:

Praised be to you, my Lord, with all your creatures, especially Sir Brother Sun . . . Praised be to you, my Lord, through Sister Moon and the Stars . . . Praised be to you, my Lord, through Brother Wind, and through the Air, cloudy and serene, and every kind of weather . . . Praised be to you, my Lord, through Sister Water . . . through Brother Fire . . . through our Sister, Mother Earth . . .

This spiritual theology in which a communion with nature is celebrated has become a target for some harsh criticism and censure. Francis has been condemned as a pantheist. The Judeo-Christian tradition has always maintained that while God dwells in the created order (divine immanence), God is also wholly other (divine transcendence). Those who hold to pantheism reject the idea that God is transcendent. For them, God is everything and everything is God. But Francis was no pantheist. As Joe Nangle puts it, one should rather think of him as a contemplative, since "he saw the handprint of the Divine in all of nature."[8]

What do we need, then, in order to experience this deep connection with nature that is productive both of inner healing and care of the environment? Clearly, we need to break out of the shackles that Cartesian thought has put us in. We need to see ourselves as living in kinship with the natural world. We need to have this vision, but we also need to live it out. What animates our relationship with nature—and indeed all of our relationships for that matter—is eros.[9] Webster's Dictionary uses the following terms to describe this form of love: "ardent desire," "yearning," and "aspiring self-fulfilling love often having a sensuous quality." Eros is a desire, but it is not limited to sexual desire. It is "a creative energy, the life force, the unifier, the creative urge in nature and the human spirit . . ."[10] In Greek philosophy, it is construed as the desire, the drive, to participate fully in knowledge and in the good. For St. Augustine, it is the power that drives people toward God. "My heart is restless," he wrote in the *Confessions,* "and it will not rest until it rests in you." Eros, in the most general sense, is a desire, an urging force that connects us to that which is of ultimate value for us. The passion of eros pulls us toward the beloved, knowledge, God, and—related to our current interest—nature. Eros is the power of unity in the created order. The person breathing in the spiritual energy of the natural world is filled with eros.

THE SPIRIT OF THE CITY

In singing the praises of nature as a locus for spiritual attunement and renewal, I do not mean to give the impression that God is nowhere to be found in the city. The city is, along with all of creation, the domain of God. As we walk about a typical city, what do we see? We see, sometimes, the isolation of city life. People rush by and little or no contact is made. In the film *Crocodile Dundee,* Australian Paul Hogan makes this fact an opportunity for humor. Hogan's character, Mick Dundee, is accustomed to country life where strangers still greet each other and even stop and have a leisurely chat. Not realizing that the context is altogether different, Mick tries to engage with New Yorkers as they rush to their next commitment. They are, of course, thoroughly bemused.

How can we make connections with our fellow city-dwellers? Certainly we are not as naive as Mick Dundee. But yet we do want to personalize our city experience. Martin Buber is famous for his poetic exposition of the I-Thou encounter. In this encounter, two people make themselves present to each other. In a world where people are often made into objects, Buber pleads for the establishment of intersubjectivity. He is not only speaking about deep and meaningful conversations, but also about the significant glance exchanged between two strangers. Two commuters, for example, can connect through a warm look even though no words are exchanged. Or we can go a step further. I remember Professor Frank Andersen, an Old Testament scholar and an Anglican priest, telling me that he always made use of the name tags supermarket checkout operators use. This was one way he tried to overcome the anonymity of city life.

In the city we also see people who have lost their purpose in life, who are no longer coping, who are existing rather than really living. Perhaps they, like the Son of Man, have nowhere to lay their heads at night. How do we respond? Do we take the time to talk with them? Do we pass on by? Do we allow this immediate contact with others who are suffering deeply to challenge us and to reshape the way that we engage with the world around us?

At the other end of the spectrum, we also find in the city the glittering superstructures where all the latest and greatest goods are available for consumption. Consumerism has become a rival of the more established religions in the modern world. There is much to be lamented about the prominent place shopping malls have in modern life. But this should be balanced with a reference to the benefits they confer. Robert Banks expresses it this way:

> Shopping malls are the new cathedrals of the suburbs, increasingly dominating the geography, road networks, socialising and politics of local communities. Economic considerations dominate these complexes and big companies control much of what goes on inside of them. Yet to some extent such malls do provide space for people to gather and for communal activities to take place . . . Buying and selling are also valid activities in themselves and have helped improve not just the quantity but also the quality of life in certain respects.[11]

Shopping provides another opportunity for an I-Thou moment between strangers. I have sometimes, for example, experienced a bond, loose but yet significant, with a saleswoman when selecting a present for my wife. I most often don't want help from the sales staff; I prefer the freedom of browsing on my own. But when I am shopping for items that I know very little about—those that my wife would appreciate—I value assistance. If the saleswoman has been helpful and interested, I have had the sense of working together on a common project. Having found the right gift, there has been for both of us a sense of joy in achieving our goal, and more importantly, in anticipating the pleasure that the gift will bring. To be sure, given that the

saleswoman didn't know my wife, her joy was small in comparison
to mine. But nonetheless, she experienced satisfaction in helping me
find the right gift to express my love for my wife. In this very ordinary experience, there was a meeting between an I and a Thou, and
the Spirit of God was truly present.

A SPIRITUALITY OF TIME

My family and I lived for a few years in Glenalta in the Adelaide
Hills of South Australia. One of the things that attracted us to that
place is the fact that the Belair National Park is so close. We envisioned numerous family outings in the beauty and splendor of the
park. On one of our walks in the park, my wife and I noticed the excellent barbecue facilities that are provided. We discussed the idea of
a weekly family barbecue in the park. It will take us out of the busyness of life, we reflected, and create a small oasis amid the aridity of
the weekly routine. But alas, the walks were few and far between, and
the barbecue plan remained just an idea. Time for many of us has become a tyrant. Or, to change the metaphor, there is a new poverty for
many in the modern industrialized nations. The term "a new poverty"
comes from Robert Banks:

> [A] new poverty has emerged in societies like our own over the
> last two centuries. It is a poverty of the affluent rather than one
> that is immediately recognisable. While a few groups have suf-
> fered as a result of this poverty before, it has never occurred on a
> mass scale as is happening now. We may not be poor economi-
> cally as the majority of people are in the Two-thirds World, but
> we are poor in terms of time, whereas they tend to have an abun-
> dance of it. What we have gained in terms of material things, we
> have lost in terms of disposable time.[12]

To redeem one's time in the face of constant demands is a major
challenge. It requires at least two personal capacities. First, we need a
capacity to hear God as we ask God to show us the priorities that need
to be established in our lives. There are almost countless ways in
which we can use our time. We are confronted continually with opportunities for work and service outside of our day jobs. If we are to

redeem our time, we need to prayerfully establish those opportunities that will be taken up, and those that will be passed by.

In letting certain possibilities go, and this brings me to the second capacity, we need to be able to say "no." The degree of difficulty we experience in declining requests from others is a barometer of our personal and spiritual development. If we find ourselves too often saying "yes" when we really want to say "no," we need to ask why this is the case. There are all kinds of possible reasons. It could be, for instance, that the inability to decline a request indicates low self-esteem. The fact that the other person may be disappointed is too much to bear for a person with a fragile sense of self. Saying "yes" makes us popular. The other person is always very pleased to find a willing agent. Conversely, when the person approached turns down the invitation, there is disappointment. And some persons are more expressive of their disappointment than others. Some are even ungracious, or manipulative, or both of these things. It takes a strong sense of self-worth to decline in that context.

The reason for finding it difficult to say "no" could be quite different. It could be that one is addicted to achievement. It is good to be passionate about our projects; it is laudable to work hard at them; and there are times when circumstances will require us to work harder than we would like. But we know that it is not good to be driven to achieve. Drivenness is a sign of psychological and spiritual ill health. Responding to the challenge of the poverty of time is a central concern in the spiritual life. Time is a precious commodity, and the disciples of Christ are required to use it efficiently. We are to use our hours efficiently, but we should not be stingy with them. I believe that God wants us to sometimes "waste" time. To simply spend a few hours walking and being with God might seem to some to be a luxury that can be ill afforded in a world with so many demands and so many opportunities for mission and service. But it is a "luxury," I suggest, that God wants us to have. God wants us to have it because God knows that we need it. Quite apart from making time for the "useless" activity of prayer, to occasionally fritter away a few hours in mindless activities is, I believe, something that is blessed by God. A life in which every moment must be filled with meaningful mental, physical, and spiritual activity is too terrible to contemplate. There is a joy in disciplining oneself only if one can occasionally relax and cast off the pressures of time and responsibilities. Using our time well means being responsible without becoming neurotic!

One area of our lives for which we certainly need to make time is family life. For those of us who have both a public and a private role, the problem that we face is that by the time we get to our loved ones, we are often almost worn out. Living out our dual vocation is extremely challenging and demanding. It is here that our spirituality is both tested and formed.

SPIRITUALITY IN MARRIAGE AND FAMILY

During the twentieth century, we saw enormous changes in the way marriage and family life was understood and actualized.[13] The traditional model involving a head-complement relationship was supplanted by a senior partner-junior partner paradigm. More recently, we have witnessed a growing number of married people opting for an equal-partner marriage. In this new model, the emphasis is on companionship, mutuality, and shared work. The driving force behind the move to equality in marriage was the women's movement. Women rightly spoke out against the previously unquestioned assumption that men should be head or even senior partner in the household.

The limited access that women traditionally had to public life was also strongly challenged by feminists. Women began entering the workforce in large numbers from the 1950s onward. There are now only about 8 percent of American families that follow the traditional pattern according to which the husband is the sole breadwinner and the wife stays at home to care for the children and to manage the household. Most women today have both a private and a public role. From a Christian perspective, this is not something to be lamented— quite the opposite. Roman Catholic theologian and mother of three Julie Hanlon Rubio rightly argues that a dual vocation is appropriate for Christian parents. Discipleship, she points out, is the context in which the calling of Christian parents should be situated:

> Scripture scholars tell us that discipleship is the fundamental calling of Christians, and this presumes a public vocation. Certainly one can practice virtue, keep many commandments of the Old and New testaments, and obey God's will at home in one's

family . . . However, one cannot . . . fully realize the demands of discipleship to Jesus of Nazareth unless one also has a public vocation.[14]

In the old model—head and complement—the locus of authority, the pattern of decision making, and the division of labor were all quite clearly established. The head would consult with his complement, but he assumed final responsibility for making important family decisions. Further, he was not expected to make much of a contribution to the care of the children, and even less to the cooking, cleaning, and washing chores. He would, however, take care of home maintenance work and financial affairs, and would usually assume a significant level of responsibility in disciplining the children. One might say that the situation was "black and white" in relation to the ordering of marriage and family life. Both parties were clear about their roles and responsibilities. The new model in which the partners are equal, on the other hand, has taken us into a gray area. We are not quite sure what constitutes a fair thing anymore. We are also not clear on what the criteria should be for making decisions. How do the partners prioritize needs and desires? In the case of two full-time working parents, how do they decide what is a fair distribution of tasks? If a decision is made that both partners working full-time is putting too much pressure on family life, how will a reduction in hours be worked out? Will it be the husband or the wife who seeks a cutback in hours, or a new part-time job? On what basis is such a decision to be made? It would be fairer if both partners opted for part-time work. But this is not financially feasible for most families. What about the situation in which one partner gets offered a better job in another town or city? The decision to accept the offer or to turn it down is most often very difficult.

The new family paradigm has taken us into murky waters. Or to use the metaphor developed in the previous paragraph, the equal-partner marriage is lived out, partially at least, in the gray zone. The question that is central in a spirituality of the everyday is especially prominent for those who occupy this zone of uncertainty and confusion. Living in the gray zone, we need to ask with some urgency: "What are you asking of me, of us, in this ambiguous situation, O God?" We also find ourselves praying with real intensity: "Guide us through this murky middle ground, Spirit Friend."

Let me offer two stories of personal struggle that highlight the challenges and opportunities associated with a spirituality of the gray zone. The first comes from Bonnie Miller-McLemore. In her book *Also a Mother,* she tells us just how difficult it has been for her to enact her dual vocation of mother and theologian.[15] It was not a matter of her and husband, Mark, picking up a manual on how to faithfully live through the tensions associated with the combined vocations of parent and professional person. There is not one. Together Bonnie and Mark learned "the complicated lessons" that are associated with life in that gray zone that is mutuality in a married partnership:

> We discovered that the mutuality we wanted to maintain could not be spelled out as easily as kitchen duty, but required a measured and steady response to the continually emerging, evolving needs of our children for love, and our needs to love ourselves as parents and otherwise. Actualizing this mutuality amidst the flux and disparities between us required compensation for the person who had given too much. It required flexibility, improvisation, and support. Daily, we tried to find ways to balance the inequities of the demands that my physical proximity created for both of us, and to build avenues for common participation, often with little outside encouragement or support. This sometimes meant intentionally inverting and overriding what seemed our natural impulses. When it seemed right and necessary, it even meant overriding the real physical inclinations of the "gut" with an affirmation of the deeper realities which our socialization had denied us—Mark's physical experience of the lure of our children and my experience of a desire for creative work.[16]

The extent to which Bonnie and Mark had to break new ground is indicated through the reference to intentionally overriding natural impulses. They set about reaching beyond the tendencies set in place by the socialization process to embrace "deeper realities." What is described is truly an adventure of the spirit.

The second story relates to a significant struggle that my wife, Janelle, and I found ourselves caught in a few years ago. After being granted my doctoral degree in the pastoral care and counseling area, I was fortunate enough to obtain a lecturing job in Parkin-Wesley College and the School of Theology at Flinders University. In a word, the experience was absolutely brilliant. I found myself very much in love with the work and with those connected with it. I also really enjoyed living in the city of Adelaide. We had a lovely home set in the foothills, and the lifestyle associated with the city felt very right to me. Life was as close to perfect as any person could want.

In the second year of our stay in Adelaide, however, it became very obvious that Janelle was feeling quite different from how I felt. She did not find life in Adelaide "perfect" at all. In fact, she was experiencing a need to return home to southeast Queensland. We talked about it of course, but Janelle never took it as far as to ask me to resign from my job. By the middle of our third year, however, the urge to go home was so strong that Janelle could no longer push it aside. It was clear that a decision had to be made.

What we found really difficult was the fact that, first, there was no clear principle that we could grasp hold of to help us determine what was fair, and second, that there was no possibility of compromise. As hard as we prayed, and as earnestly and honestly as we discussed, we kept coming back to the same point. For us, the problem boiled down to the fact that, on the one hand, I loved my job and was unlikely to get a similar job in Brisbane (at least in the foreseeable future), and on the other, that it was very important for Janelle to return home. We also found ourselves knocking up against a brick wall as we searched for a compromise. Janelle considered that frequent trips home would not be sufficient. Her need went beyond catching up with friends and family; she wanted to reestablish our family life in her hometown, Brisbane. For my part, while I was prepared to consider arranging my week around four days in Adelaide and three in Brisbane, it was clear that such an arrangement would send us very quickly to the bankruptcy courts.

So, no compromise and no way of establishing what is fair in the situation. We both had valid needs and desires; someone had to make a sacrifice. The question that is the key one in a spirituality of the everyday was written large before Janelle and me both: "What are you asking of me in this situation, O God?" For a very long time, no clear answer was forthcoming. The turning point for me came when I found myself saying to a colleague, "For whatever reason, it just doesn't feel right to say to Janelle, 'I'm sorry, but I just can't give up this job.'" My colleague responded by saying, "Why not?" As I thought about her question to me, I realized that my love of the job and my deep reluctance to give it up was stopping me from accepting what I knew in my depths to be true. Janelle had been prepared in the past to make sacrifices to help me actualize my hopes and dreams; now it was my turn.

Life in the gray zone stretches us enormously; it facilitates a significant movement forward in our discipleship. The growth and development that occurs in and through family life, it is important to recognize, is ultimately not for the individual members alone. Family life provides us with resources that are to be made available for service in the Realm of God. We are called to cooperate with God in God's work of bringing new life, healing, and wholeness to the world. Leroy Howe expresses it well:

> From a Christian perspective, in God-centered families the wide range of supportive, problem-solving, and growth-enhancing resources their members have available to them exist for a larger purpose, the purpose of forming a spirit of enthusiastic cooperativeness and readiness for relationships outside the family, relationships characterized by mutual cherishing and self-giving, and by a shared vision of a better world for everyone built upon partnerships between people grateful to be called by God to God's service.[17]

SPIRITUALITY AND PUBLIC LIFE

As we have seen, it is important to recognize that our close personal relationships need to be viewed in the context of our wider experience of life and the world. Though our intimate relationships are central in the life of the spirit, we need to broaden our horizon of engagement. From the inner circle, our love must extend outwards into the public realm. Elizabeth Dreyer articulates well the need to move beyond a privatized spirituality:

> A privatized spirituality too often leads to a stifled conscience. One test of a healthy spiritual life is the gradual expansion of our hearts to embrace the world. The expression of care and compassion within our families and in our relationships with friends

and colleagues slowly and gradually extends its horizons to include those in the next town or country; those "others" who are different from us in race, sex, age and religion; and even those who have offended us or done us harm. Our love for the world cannot thrive without justice. Our love leads us to be concerned about how society is organized, how wealth, power, privileges, rights and responsibilities are distributed on every level—local, national and global. And the quality of our justice is tested by the ways in which we work to protect the poor and marginalized.[18]

In seeking to extend the horizon of our love through pursuing justice, we find ourselves, it goes without saying, facing risk and searching for courage. One reason for this is that an involvement in justice issues plunges one into a state of ambiguity (the gray zone again). On the one hand, there is the fact that it is often not easy to identify exactly where justice is to be found in a particular situation or dispute. It is most often not the case that the parties involved fall neatly into the categories of oppressor and oppressed. I remember well the South East Queensland Electricity Board (SEQEB) dispute in the early 1980s. It is not necessary to go into all the details here. The essence of the dispute was that the electricity workers had for a number of years been running a series of power disruptions to further their claims for better pay and conditions. Naturally, the blackouts caused considerable inconvenience to householders and resulted in large losses for many businesses. Finally, the Premier at the time, Joh Bjelke-Peterson, issued an ultimatum: Either stop the disruptions or face the sack. The blackouts continued and 1,000 workers were sacked, and they were denied superannuation entitlements. At the time I was a theological student, and those of us in the Ministry and Mission course were asked to reflect theologically on the dispute and submit a paper. While I felt strongly that the Premier had profoundly abused his power in ordering the sackings, I also wrestled with the fact that the electricity workers also had considerable power and had used it quite aggressively on a number of occasions to promote their cause. While I was clear about the fact that the sackings represented an extreme and unacceptable response, I had little idea, given the repeated failure of negotiations, as to how the government might have more constructively and justly countered the SEQEB workers' misuse of their power.

Going through the exercise made me very much aware of the level of ambiguity that is often associated with sociopolitical disputation.

What often happens when a person is confronted with the fact that there are rights and wrongs on both sides is that she finds it very difficult to choose a side in the dispute. It is tempting to endlessly analyze and reflect on the situation in a desperate attempt to find clarity. Such an approach usually puts a person into a state of paralysis. She is unable to act. Neutrality is not an option, however. In the end, sitting on the fence can only be seen as an immoral action. Archbishop Desmond Tutu makes this very clear when he writes:

> If you are neutral in a situation of injustice, you have chosen the side of the oppressor. If an elephant has his foot on the tail of the mouse, and you say you are neutral, the mouse will not appreciate your neutrality.[19]

Ambiguity is also present in relation to working with the other persons in the justice network. He or she may, for example, be advocating views and actions that are much more radical than one feels comfortable with. To illustrate, let me again use a personal experience. I recall joining in a Palm Sunday peace march and rally some years ago. While many of the speakers at the rally were espousing views that I could quite readily align myself with, I felt distinctly uncomfortable with the comments made by those speakers with socialist commitments. The cause of peace and justice is promoted by a rainbow coalition, and sometimes we find ourselves wishing that the spectrum were quite a bit narrower! Coping with its breadth stretches us emotionally and spiritually. To stand back and endlessly analyze and debate is tempting; what is required is a risky plunge into action.

Another major reason that risk and courage loom large is that in joining a justice coalition you may become a target for suspicion and even vilification within the church and the community. Most of us value popularity and respectability. To champion an unpopular cause demands much of us; it asks for substantial inner fortitude.

Even these cursory comments will be enough to highlight the fact that engagement with public issues represents huge personal challenges. Not only is there the challenge to love, but we are also stretched in our capacity for risk and courage. There are clearly very significant opportunities for personal and spiritual growth associated with a justice ministry.

SUMMARY

I have been quite selective in this discussion of the spirituality of the everyday. There are quite a few other areas that could have been addressed. But my aim was not to be comprehensive, but rather to illustrate the potential for personal and spiritual growth to be found in the common experiences of life.

In the new approach to spirituality, we are encouraged to wait upon the Spirit in the ordinary stuff of life. The spiritual way is not so much about drawing away from the world, as important as this sometimes is, but rather about attending to the whispers of God in the midst of everyday life.

Chapter 6

Conversion to the True Self

In Chapter 5, we reflected on the way our spirituality is expressed in the everyday world. As we engage in the daily round, we encounter a range of opportunities for conversion to Christ. There are those who think of conversion in terms of a discrete event located at a particular point in time. Indeed, this can be an important dimension in the conversion experience. Many people can point to a particular period, if not a certain day, when they made a decision to respond to God's gracious offer of healing and liberation in Christ. But, of course, conversion is a process. Is there ever a time when one can say that one is fully and completely converted to the way of Christ? We are people on the way. We are journeying out of the darkness into the light. Sometimes, we allow ourselves to slip back into the shadows. Christ is calling us ever onwards to live as people of the light.

I aim here to map a particular territory of conversion. It is the great spiritual writer and Trappist monk, Thomas Merton, who shows so clearly and incisively that the most crucial conversion in the spiritual life is from the false to the true self. To grow into the true self, we must conform ourselves ever more closely to Christ. Indeed, we must allow Christ to establish himself as our "superior self." In the first part of our journey, we will reflect on this vitally important spiritual task.

In the second stage of mapping conversion, I will describe a process of prayer that supports movement toward the true self. This process is what might be called "storied" prayer. A good story takes us back into the past ("Once upon a time . . ."); it engages us by bringing the plot into our present; and it projects a hopeful future ("And they all lived happily ever after . . ."). In a similar way, a prayer life that

Moving Toward Spiritual Maturity
© 2007 by The Haworth Press, Inc. All rights reserved.
doi:10.1300/5886_06

supports conversion needs a past, present, and future tense. Through prayer we can allow Jesus to take us into the joy and the pain of our personal histories and allow him to heal and renew us. In the present moment, our prayerfulness helps us to be attentive to the movement of the world around us. As we attend to this world, we sense God calling us into new possibilities for faithful living. To attend in this way is necessarily to open ourselves to the future. God is asking us through our prayerful reflection on present experience to choose a future self. This self will be in continuity with the past self, but will also include a new dimension. In this way, three forms of prayer will be developed: *remembering, attending,* and *choosing.* Let us begin by reflecting on the vitally important issue of the true self.

TRUE AND FALSE SELVES

We virtually never feel 100 percent ourselves. The novelist Walker Percy brings this sad reality home to us in a most striking way by pointing out that while we humans usually feel only about 50 percent ourselves, a cat lazing in the sun is completely at home with itself.[1] Percy confronts us with this telling experience of Will Barrett, the hero of his book *The Second Coming:*

> As he sat gazing at the cat, he saw all at once what had gone wrong, wrong with people, with him, not with the cat—saw it with the smiling certitude with which Einstein is said to have hit upon his famous theory in the act of boarding a streetcar in Zurich . . . Sitting there in the sun with its needs satisfied, . . . the cat was exactly a hundred percent, no more no less. As for Will Barrett, as for people nowadays—they were never a hundred percent themselves. They occupied a place uneasily more or less successfully. More likely they were forty-seven percent themselves, or rarely, as in the case of Einstein on the streetcar, three hundred percent. All too often these days they were two percent, spectators, who hardly occupied a place at all.[2]

What Percy is highlighting for us in his own unique way is the fact that to live is to encounter within oneself confusion, doubt, frustration, alienation, deception, and disappointment. In a word, to live is to struggle. Alan Jones helpfully characterizes this struggle through the metaphor of the duel.[3] We have dueling selves. The duel is over the struggle for freedom. Are we lords or are we slaves? That is the key question for anyone who wants to grow into psychospiritual wholeness.

We have seen (Chapter 3) that for Paul it is the "law of sin" that keeps the "inmost self" in bondage. He constantly experiences defeat in his intention to live according to God's will, with the result that he becomes a prisoner to this law:

> In my inmost self I dearly love God's law, but I see that acting on my body there is a different law which battles against the law in my mind. So I am brought to be prisoner of that law of sin which lives inside my body. (Rom 7: 22-23)

Paul recognizes very clearly that he lives with inner opposites. There is a duel going on. The inmost self represents the self that is oriented to God's will. Over against this self is the law of sin.

Thomas Merton uses the language of true and false selves to help us understand what is at stake in the psychospiritual duel that is at the heart of human existence. The struggle to establish the true self is something that Merton wrestled with for most of his life. In turning to his various treatments of the subject, one opens up a treasure chest of spiritual wisdom. The essential aim of spiritual life is union with God in Christ. To experience this loving union, Merton observes, is to experience profound joy: "The only true joy on earth is to escape from the prison of our own selfhood . . . and enter by love into union with the Life who dwells and sings within the essence of every creature and in the core of our own souls."[4] In drawing close to God, the Christian both comes to know the divine will and is empowered to live it out. To know God and God's will is to come to one's true self. To refuse the divine life and purpose is to contradict oneself. This self-contradiction that characterizes the false self is the result of sin.

> To say I was born in sin is to say I came into the world with a false self. I came into existence under a sign of contradiction, being someone that I was never intended to be and therefore a denial of what I am supposed to be.[5]

Every one of us, says Merton, is "shadowed" by an illusory person. It is an illusion to believe that one can live outside God's will. An attempt to do so puts a person outside reality, outside life.

The motive forces behind the illusion are pride, egoism, and self-assertion. A person thinks of herself as a "completely free autonomous self, with unlimited possibilities."[6] She acts as if she is a god, with everything within her reach. Such a person thinks that she is truly free, but the truth, says Merton, is that she is gripped by a "psychic and spiritual cramp."[7]

Every person has a tendency to pride and self-assertion. Everyone suffers from an inner cramp. It is through prayer and contemplation, observes Merton, that one is able to free it up. In coming before God in a spirit of poverty, honesty, and openness, a person comes to see the ego and the trickery of the false self.

> [T]he dimensions of prayer in solitude are those of man's ordinary anguish, his self-searching, his moments of nausea at his own vanity, falsity and capacity for betrayal. Far from establishing one in an unassailable narcissistic security, the way of prayer brings us face to face with the sham and indignity of the false self . . .[8]

We saw that Merton connects the false self to a tendency to see oneself as a god. In *The New Man* (1961), a new image appears. The picture shifts from striving to be like God to attempting to steal from God. Echoing Prometheus, the false self tries to steal life and meaning from God. In a perverse manner, the Promethean self thinks that her spiritual perfection is something that God wants to stop her from attaining. She resorts to stealing her fire from heaven. She should be focused on God's glory; instead she is preoccupied with her own perfection. Merton finds here the image of humanity's psychological situation. We are "guilty, rebellious, frustrated, unsure of [ourselves], of [our] gifts and of [our] own strength, alienated, yet seeking to assert [ourselves]."[9]

The twin problems are pride and egoism, and like a dog chasing its tail they draw us into a circle of emptiness and futility. "[P]ride is simply a form of supreme and absolute subjectivity. It sees all things from the viewpoint of a limited, individual self that is constituted as the center of the universe."[10] Pride and selfishness, when they go un-checked, suck a person into a world of ever-decreasing proportions. In the end, this world is empty and meaningless. Life and meaning are found only when one is hidden in Christ. In drawing near to Christ I find myself and all that I need to be fully alive given freely to me. Pride stops me from opening myself to this grace.

In his later writings, Merton employs the existentialist notion of dread to illumine the nature of this willful turning away from God. The truth of a person's life is given to him or her by God. Dread is symptomatic of a turning away from that truth. "It is the deep, con-fused, metaphysical awareness of a *basic antagonism between the self and God* due to estrangement from him by perverse attachment to a 'self' which is mysterious and illusory" (emphasis in the original).[11]

Dread serves a positive purpose in the spiritual life.[12] If one is at-tentive to it, it points one to God and God's grace. It reminds a person that ultimately life in this world is an insecure one. Attending to this psychic and spiritual signal reminds her that everything that is "hers"—her wisdom, her virtue, her intelligence, and her talents—cannot be relied on in any ultimate sense. Dread reminds her of her nothingness and directs her to fullness in God. In losing oneself, one finds God.

In order to lose oneself, one must embrace a spiritual poverty. Hu-mility, Merton stresses time and again, is the condition of the possi-bility of coming to one's true self. In humbling myself I experience true freedom.[13] It is the freedom of finally finding myself in God. This is my first and last task. "[T]here is only one problem on which all my existence, my peace and my happiness depend: to discover myself in discovering God. If I find Him, I will find myself; and if I find my true self, I will find Him."[14]

In finding God, a person is drawn into the sphere of the divine mis-sions.[15] God the Source (the Father), dwelling in her personal depths, communicates to her the Word and the Spirit. In this way, God lives in her not only as her Creator, but also as "[her] other and true self."[16] Merton turns frequently to Paul's expression to communicate this state of being: "It is no longer I who live, but Christ who lives in me." With this in mind, Merton tells us that Christ becomes one's "supe-rior self."[17] Christ has united the faithful one's inmost self with his own life. In this way, she becomes a new being, a new person in

Christ. Mysteriously, Christ living in her remains himself, but at the same time he becomes her true self. From the moment that a person is united to Christ, says Merton, there is "no longer any contradiction" in the fact that they are different persons.[18]

All of this has the form of a gift. The change of heart that is required to break free of the illusory self and to turn to God is a work of grace. God graciously offers us the joy and peace that comes with finding our true selves. We can break free of the crippling effects of pride and egoism. The gift is freely given, but there are surprisingly few takers. This is not God's fault, Merton points out, but ours.

> [I]f the gift be rare, it is not because of any niggardliness on the part of an infinitely liberal God. It is because of our fear, our blindness, our ignorance, and our hatred of risk. For after all, in order to make this leap out of ourselves we have to be willing to let go of everything that is our own—all our own plans, all our own hesitations, all our own judgments.[19]

Merton laments the fact that relatively few people are ready for the spiritual poverty that leads into fullness of life in Christ. Self-realization is freely available, but it is not cheap.

In reviewing what has been presented so far, it might seem that Merton has two unfortunate tendencies. A tendency, first, to shrink the Christian life down to private experience is evident. We can also discern a leaning toward a pessimistic view of the world. The mature Merton, however, developed a much broader understanding. He continued to stress the centrality of love and fidelity in discipleship. However, the arena for the expression of these virtues is no longer simply interpersonal relations; it also includes sociopolitical life. In *Conjectures of a Guilty Bystander* (1966), living out of one's true self means orienting oneself to "an objective moral good" and rejecting the norms of a society that wants to believe it is good but which in reality too often promotes injustice and evil.

Indicated here is a fundamental change in Merton's way of understanding "the world." The world is still the symbol of sin, but its failure is expressed more broadly. No longer are people seen by Merton to fail simply in the personal realm of passion, power, and pride; our failure is drawn into the arena of sociopolitical life. The enemies of truth and genuine freedom are totalitarianism, the cult of technology and consumption, the warring spirit, and the greed and inequality that are behind world hunger. Collectively, says Merton, we have bought a lie. The false self is a symptom of a mass illness. To be cured, we will need to decontaminate our minds.

> The greatest need of our time is to clean out the enormous mass of mental and emotional rubbish that clutters our minds and makes of all political and social life a mass illness. Without this housecleaning we cannot begin to *see*.[20]

Merton's understanding of the world changed in another direction as well. As we have seen, the view of the world that he presents in *Seeds of Contemplation* (1949) is quite gloomy. It is the locus of pride, passion, and self-assertion. This view clashes with the more incarnational theology that is popular today.[21] While it is recognized in this theology that there is a dark side in all of us and in the socioeconomic and political systems we create together, nevertheless the fact that God assumed flesh and lived among us constitutes an affirmation of our humanness. This "yes" to human existence that God utters in and through Christ was not on Merton's horizon when he wrote *Seeds*. As a result, he was for a long time branded as the voice of *contemptus mundi*. "[D]ue to a book I wrote thirty years ago," he reflects in *Contemplation in a World of Action,*

> I have myself become a sort of stereotype of the world-denying contemplative—the man who spurned New York, spat on Chicago, and tromped on Louiseville, heading for the woods with Thoreau in one pocket, John of the Cross in another, and holding the Bible open at the Apocalypse.[22]

In that work, as in his other later writings, we see the call for the Christian to maintain openness to the world. Jesus rejected the sin of the world, but did not thereby reject the world outright. He loved the world and gave his life to redeem it. The later Merton sees any suggestion that the Christian must choose either Christ or the world as wrongly conceived. Rather, "we choose Christ by choosing the world as it really is in him, that is to say, created and redeemed by him, and encountered in the ground of our own personal freedom and love."[23] The world is not a problem, Merton contends, if we see that the grace and redeeming love of God makes Christ, the world, one's sister/ brother, and one's true self one and the same.[24]

This change in Merton's outlook fits well with the perspective developed in the previous chapter. Christians are not called to turn their backs on the world. The truly spiritual person is not the one who retreats into a sheltered place. It is in the common experiences of life in the world that we hear God and follow God's lead toward the true self.

Henri Nouwen picks up on this theme of hearing God in the everyday world in much of his writing. He talks about the conversion to the true self (though he does not use this phrase) in terms of three fundamental movements: from *loneliness to solitude,* from *hostility to hospitality,* and from *illusion to prayer.*[25] To move into solitude, hospitality, and prayer is to take major strides on the path to conversion to Christ's way. In fact, these three spiritual states cannot simply be placed alongside each other. It is the life of prayer that makes solitude and hospitality possible. In order for us to find the true way of prayer, we must let go of our illusions. This is strongly reminiscent of Merton's view of spiritual life. The false self is an illusory self. It is the side of a person that looks at life, the self, and God in a distorted way. It therefore lives through illusion. In entering into the discipline of prayer and contemplation, truth begins to take over the territory occupied by falsity.

We fall into illusion, Nouwen observes, when we attempt to eternalize ourselves and the world. It may seem strange at first sight to talk about an illusion of immortality. Surely every sane person knows that he or she cannot live forever. And yet, many people mentally construct their world as if it is permanent. If this is not the case, why do they live as if everything depends on the material complex that they are assembling? Indeed, it is this illusion that allows them to keep the mystery and the awesomeness of death at arm's length—at least for a time. One is reminded here of Ernest Becker's thesis in his book, *The Denial of Death.*[26] Becker refers to a denial that is expressed through the heroic attempt to "immortalize" the self by divinizing an earthly object or project. The reality of death is pushed into the background as we allow our daily tasks to consume us. We keep our existential angst at bay by focusing all our energies on the project at hand.

Another common illusion is our almost universal tendency to create God in our own image. That is, we want God to look like us because in this way we achieve a god that we can manage. When we allow God to be God, on the other hand, we run the risk of having to live a risky existence. So we need to ask ourselves, Nouwen observes, whether we want to live in a world that we construct, or in the world that God is building. And the world that God is building is one in which solitude and hospitality have a special place. "When we move from illusion to prayer, we move from the human shelter to the house of God. It is there that our solitude as well as our hospitality can be sustained."[27]

There is no way that we can live in solitude and hospitality without communion with God. But what exactly is solitude? It sounds as though Nouwen is advocating a monkish retreat from the world. In fact, he is talking about an experience that is possible right in the middle of the hustle and bustle of city life. The solitude that he is referring to is a capacity to listen for the voice of God in one's innermost self. A lonely person, in contrast, is dead scared of quiet moments alone. To be alone means having to live with questions, when what she really wants is the answers that will settle her disquiet. But these are not the answers the Spirit brings out of the solitude, but rather the easy, ready-made answers that others are only too willing to supply. Those who are not afraid of solitude are ready to pay attention to the true self. When we fail to create this authentic inner space, however, the false self takes over:

> Without the solitude of heart, the intimacy of friendship, marriage and community life cannot be creative. Without the solitude of heart, our relationships with others easily become needy and greedy, sticky and clinging, dependent and sentimental, exploitative and parasitic, because without the solitude of heart we cannot experience the others as different from ourselves but only as a people who can be used for the fulfillment of our own, often hidden, needs.[28]

While most of us can relate quite readily to the tendency to retreat from a conversation with the inner self, some of us may feel that in talking about hostility Nouwen is talking about someone else. We are, after all, gentle, peace-loving souls. While that may for the most part be perfectly true, can we not also recall times when we have engaged another side, a darker side, of the self? When we have been attacked, have we not been tempted to hit back? There we were, formulating the words that would put our enemy in his or her place once and for all. Or think about the tendency to become jealous and competitive. When others talk about their successes, we often envy rather than celebrate with them. Finally, there is always before us a tendency to host others on our terms. We don't really want them to be themselves; we would prefer that they conform to our rules and expectations. This is hostility rather than hospitality. A good host creates a warm, welcoming space where the guests feel free and at home.

> The paradox of hospitality is that it wants to create emptiness, not a fearful emptiness, but a friendly emptiness where strangers can enter and discover themselves as created free; free to sing their own songs, speak their own languages, dance their own dances. . . . Hospitality is not a subtle invitation to adopt the life style of the host, but the gift of a chance for the guest to find his own.[29]

We saw that along with the private face of the false self there is also the public one. In my country, Australia, many of us are deeply saddened, angered, and shamed by the "fearful emptiness" that we have been creating through our "border protection" policy. As a nation we are so gripped by the fear of being overrun by refugees that we happily hold men, women, and children in horribly inhospitable detention centers, and for very extended periods. The policy that is being promoted by the government builds hostility into the system in order to create a deterrent. A number of the centers are located in hot, desolate areas and the living conditions are far from adequate. The emotional violence that is being perpetrated in the name of frontier defense is, sadly, a striking example of the "mass of illness" that constitutes the social and political illusion. We are desperately in need of a conversion to the "friendly emptiness" that Nouwen talks about.

Nouwen offers incisive insights into the key movements in the conversion to the true self. This is a conversion from loneliness to solitude, from hostility to hospitality, and from illusion to prayer. And it is the third movement that is foundational. In prayer, we encounter the God of love and grace who is able to sustain us in the life of solitude and hospitality.

"STORIED PRAYER": REMEMBERING, ATTENDING, AND CHOOSING

The true self is a multifaceted reality. What we have reflected on, however, is the fact that central to an experience of it is a conversion to love, humility, solitude, and hospitality. These conversions are only possible, further, when prayer is at the heart of one's life. I suggest that the kind of prayer that leads to conversion involves three basic actions, namely, *remembering, attending,* and *choosing.* Our tendency to fall away from our calling to conform to Christ's way of love has a history. It is a history of wounding, distorted thinking, poor modeling, and a paucity of affirmation. In prayerful remembering, we can open these negative experiences to the healing grace of Christ. Along with a past, the way of conversion has a present moment. We need to attend to all the faces, scenes, and events, and ideas that we encounter in the daily round. With a praying spirit we need to inquire as to the possibilities for self-giving and hospitality that are being presented. Last, the pathway of conversion leads into the future. At certain critical points in the life of a Christian there are moments of decision making. People and circumstances make claims on us that must be answered. The challenge that gets put to us is this: Here is an opportunity for self-giving and community. Take hold of it!

Let's begin, then, with prayerful remembering. In this regard, I find David Hassel's suggestions concerning the "prayer of personal reminiscence" particularly helpful.[30] When I first came across his book on prayer and began praying through my personal history, I found it an illuminating and transformative experience. In this "historical" way of praying, one's memories are opened out into the grace of God. The understanding of memory that he works with is that of Augustine. Memories for Augustine are not simply frozen snapshots from the past, but rather a living and present reality. The events in our personal past are reshaped by current concerns and values and are available for the ongoing conversation that is the life of the self.

Hassel uses this understanding of memory, and suggests that it has a powerful part to play in forming a mature self, a self that is shaped according to the way of Christ. "To put it briefly," he writes, "prayer of personal reminiscence is a reliving of one's memories with Christ present so that the praying person can repossess his or her life in a more maturely Christian way."[31]

Margaret is one such person in need of repossessing her life. She is a middle-aged mother of two who desperately wants to relate to others in an open and mature way but finds that something blocks her. She is extremely sensitive and is always suspicious of the intentions of others. Innocuous words and actions are read as destructive intentions. Margaret responds either with verbal rebuke or with silent withdrawal. Sadly, she wants friends but so often she finds herself pushing people away. In a word, Margaret finds it very difficult to trust others. This lack of trust, not surprisingly, has a history. When she was a teenager there were violent clashes between her father and herself. Everything about her seemed to annoy her father, and he constantly made belittling comments. Having a fiery nature, she would react by unleashing a verbal tirade. He would respond in kind. Finally, her father made a decision that she had to go. It was only the strong resistance from Margaret's mother that kept her in the home until she was old enough to leave and fend for herself.

Deeply painful memories such as those Margaret lives with are never far from the surface. When Margaret reflects on her life, the clashes with her father often come to the fore. She does not force the process; the words and the images simply come. Indeed, in prayerful remembering it is important to refrain from managing the memories. It is God who raises them up.

> . . . [O]ne asks the Holy Spirit to lift into consciousness any memory which [the Spirit], not the praying person, considers important at the moment; then one asks Christ to guide the understanding of this memory; finally one asks [God] to help one to use this memory in future service . . . a service more human, full, and helpful.[32]

Hassel suggests that the prayer of personal reminiscence has four stages. In the first two, the aim is to focus only on positive memories raised up by the Holy Spirit. This puts one in a good position to deal effectively in the latter stages with memories involving pain and hurt.

In the first stage, the praying person should attend only to past experiences in which others treated her well. The reason for this is rather obvious. It is very difficult to face up to those experiences in one's life that are filled with pain, hurt, misunderstanding, and betrayal. Having rejoiced in the goodness of others and of God, one finds the strength to enter, or to reenter, one's personal history of pain and hurt. It is not only a matter of reengaging with the destructive influences of others in one's own life. When we have been hurt by others, when we have suffered under the inadequacies and failings of parents, siblings, friends, teachers, and other significant figures from our childhood and beyond, we tend to transfer some of that hurt. That is, there is a strong possibility that we will develop dysfunctional tendencies as a result of the failures in the love of others. So in looking to the toxicity in the way others have related to us, we must also consider the toxic nature of some of our encounters with others. This last set of memories is particularly difficult to face up to. Thus, in allowing the Spirit to bring up positive memories at the outset of the prayer of personal reminiscence, we are better situated to enter into the shadow memories.

In the second stage, the praying person asks God to help her focus on the memories in which she has contributed in love and self-gifting to the lives of others. That is, she brings to mind persons and situations in which she acted for the good of those involved. Now of course this may be difficult because we do not always know how we have affected others. Not everyone says, for example, "When you did so and so, it really helped me. Thank you so much." Sometimes I have experienced difficulty in finding a memory in which the other person or persons overtly expressed gratitude. At that point, I have found it helpful to recall situations in which my *intention* was very clearly to do good. We may never know how some of our words and actions have affected others, but we do know what was in our hearts at the time.

After this positive beginning, in the third stage, one begins to focus on the hurt others have caused. Hassel points out that the major difficulty here is associated with the fact that the ones who have caused us the most hurt are often the ones we have been closest to. This, I contend, is not necessarily the case. In my experience, our enemies can scar us just as deeply. In any case, because of the depth of the hurt, it will be very difficult to gain access to these memories. As Freud observed, painful memories tend to go underground. Out of conscious reach, they wreak havoc. With this in mind, Hassel makes this helpful suggestion:

> Because these resentments, often involving those dearest to a person, need to be surfaced in order to be healed by Christ, the person doing the prayer of personal reminiscence must be very trustful of the Holy Spirit and of Christ, must never forget the goodness that she or he has just witnessed in the self and others, and must be ready to accept spiritual direction and counseling if these be necessary after the resentments surface.[33]

In the fourth stage, the praying person attempts to reconnect with instances of her own destructive tendencies. As I mentioned earlier, when we suffer under failures in love by others, it is almost always the case that destructive patterns of relating begin to take shape in us. Now some of us who are overly sensitive, who tend to be overly responsible, will exaggerate the extent of the hurt that we have caused others. Some of us, those with an underdeveloped conscience, will tend to downplay the significance of the destructive words and actions. We need to seek God's help in evaluating our hurtful actions as accurately as we can. In seeking healing and forgiveness, it is clearly important to enter into the memories of personal wrongdoing in a realistic way.

I suggest that the prayer of personal reminiscence can be very significant in the formation of a mature self—a self conformed to the way of Christ. All of the experiences that one has come through—those marked by joy and celebration, along with those filled with pain and regret—have played their part in the construction of the self that one now is. In this form of prayer, we can reenter these experiences under the leading of the Holy Spirit. Not only that, but we can gain strength through contact with positive memories, and we can seek healing for the experiences of pain and hurt. To never face the past prayerfully is to ensure that buried resentments and unprocessed hurts will continue to block a movement into a life marked by love, trust, openness, and hospitality. Healing and renewal, on the other hand, is facilitated through the prayer of personal reminiscence.

The second prayer dynamic to be addressed is *attending*. For those of us who are city folk, there is noise, movement, activity, and chatter all around. We seem to be constantly on the move, and when we stop we do not enter silence, but rather another form of activity and chatter. Our lives get filled with small talk, television, and busyness. We are taken back to Nouwen's idea that we need to be converted to solitude. In solitude we reach into that inmost space where the real self speaks. When we connect with the true self, we hear God speaking most clearly.

Contemplation is a central spiritual practice. It is essential if one is to be converted to Christ's way. Contemplation is not simply for the nuns and monks of the world. Any person can step aside from the everyday demands to find quiet and solitude. Those of us who live outside the monastery must learn to look for God in the business of the daily round. What is needed is a capacity to attend to that business while remaining connected to one's quiet inner space:

> [T]he solitude that really counts is the solitude of heart; it is an inner quality or attitude that does not depend on physical isolation. On occasion this isolation is necessary to develop this solitude of heart, but it would be sad if we considered this essential aspect of the spiritual life a privilege of monks and hermits. It seems more important than ever to stress that solitude is one of the human capacities that can exist, be maintained and developed in the center of a big city, in the middle of a large crowd and in the context of a very active and productive life. A man or woman who has developed this solitude of heart is no longer pulled apart by the most divergent stimuli of the surrounding world but is able to perceive and understand this world from a quiet inner center.[34]

It is enriching and renewing from time to time to step aside from the activities and commitments that shape, direct, and sometimes even control, our lives. We need times of quietness away from the "divergent stimuli" that are omnipresent and potentially so draining. It is also true, though, that we can connect with our inmost self, with that place where God can be heard, in the midst of the daily hustle.

As we live and move through the daily round we are connected with a myriad of faces, gestures, words, sights, sounds, values, and ideologies. In attending to this heavily populated world we are confronted with the primordial wrestling of light with shadow. Here we are blessed with goodness, love, and justice; there we are assaulted by evil, aggression, and egoism. Prayerfully, from the "quiet inner center," we ask: "Loving God, how do you want me to engage with this world that I see, hear, and touch?"

This prayerful engagement in the busyness of life William Callahan calls "noisy contemplation."[35] He suggests that this style of contemplation reflects Jesus' approach. In the busy daily round of his ministry Jesus was able to connect deeply with people and with their claims on him. Through an intense "presence/awareness" Jesus was able to make his whole life a prayer. Callahan acknowledges the importance of a retreat into quietness. But he also wants to affirm the value in prayerfully being present and aware in the noise of life. Here we are listening for ways in which we might cooperate with God in God's work of loving and healing. Where there is loneliness, God is calling people to solitude. Where there is illusion, God speaks a word of truth. The hostile ones, God seeks to lead into the way of hospitality. The proud, finally, are called into the way of humility. Looking past the facade of technological and material self-confidence, God addresses the spiritual poverty. In attending to this same world in which God is extending the realm of love, truth, and justice, we need to ask the scary question: "At what points, exactly, do you want me to cooperate in your redemptive work, O God?"

We can become lost in the hurly-burly of modern life. We can submerge ourselves in a pool of chatter and small talk. We can hide from ourselves and from God by allowing ourselves to become busier and busier. The prayer of attending is about finding moments in the midst of our hectic, noisy existence to connect with God and God's redemptive program.

Attending necessarily leads into *choosing*. Connecting with my inmost center in the presence of God means that I am exposed before God. I am exposed to God speaking and calling. Having been nudged by the Spirit, I must now think hard about how, precisely, I am going to respond. Here I am confronted with the pain of discipleship. I have, perhaps, established for myself a routine that is relatively comfortable and almost predictable. Cutting in on my comfort and order is the call of God.

The call of God is always a calling onward. God is leading us into a way of discipleship that is both more expansive and more faithful. Within the disciple there is both a present self and a possible self. As we saw above, the spiritual life involves a duel. The spiritual self is a dueling self. "There is spiritual combat between the self that I am in practice and the self that I am called to be. Christ invites me to wrestle with my own character."[36]

When I attend conscientiously to the world around, it is often the case that my present self is challenged. In order to respond to the challenges the Spirit is presenting, I may need to move past the present self. It is here that a critical point is reached. Meeting God in prayer, I am asked to choose a new self. It is not, of course, that I must choose a completely new self. Rather, the term possible self is used to indicate the old or present self reshaped through certain decisive changes. This is the way of conversion.

Because this process of choosing a new self is such an uncomfortable one, solitude becomes a critical factor. One of the attractions of busyness is that it stops us from connecting with the quiet, inner self. A whirlwind of activity keeps us moving out and away from the-self-in-solitude. When we listen in quietness, we are always in danger of hearing. We may hear what God is saying. We may hear God saying that it is time to choose a new way of being in the world. Busyness keeps radical choice at bay. This is not to say that no choices are made. It is possible to be constantly choosing without ever choosing the self. Choosing a new self is a contemplative process. I must contemplate the world and my place in that world.

Contemplation is ultimately an active process. To choose a new self and then to fail to be that remade self is not to choose at all. That is why contemplation is so threatening. Having followed the Spirit's lead in prayerful reflection, the next step is implementation. In the solitude I pray, I ponder, I listen, and I hear. I hear God's voice asking me to choose. But I would much rather stay with the present self I know than choose the possible self I know not. God's call is onward and outward. Conversion to the true self involves finding the faith and the courage to choose the "real me" and the expansive life of love that I am called for. Christian songwriters John Bell and Graham Maule put this beautifully in "The Summons." God summons us to a deeper life of self-acceptance, love, and self-giving:

Will you love the "you" you hide
If I but call your name?
Will you quell the fear inside
And never be the same?
Will you use the faith you've found
To reshape the world around,
Through my sight and touch and sound
In you and you in me?*

SUMMARY

We have attended to the challenge of converting more fully to the way of Jesus. In walking this way we have journeyed more deeply into the way of love, humility, hospitality, justice, and prayer. Prayer is not simply one movement alongside the others. It is in and through prayer that the way of conversion becomes possible. In response to the exhortation to live as contemplatives, we have developed a "storied" understanding of the encounter with God. Through the steps of remembering, attending, and choosing, we provide a space for God to shape and reshape our lives. Under the sometimes gentle and sometimes strong guidance and action of the Holy Spirit, God transforms us into persons on the way of Christ in the world.

---

*Used with permission.

Chapter 7

Conversion to Compassion

In the previous chapter, we identified the conversions that we are called upon to make in order to be growing in fidelity as Christians. Central to this conversion process is an expansion in our capacity for compassionate love. "Our lives, if they are to be authentic and meaningful, must express themselves in sympathetic, unbounded love—in a word, 'compassion.'"[1] It is interesting to set this observation in the context of some of the discussions that are taking place in the wider world. The Australian political scientist, Graham Little, identifies and discusses the trend toward strong leadership in both politics and business in the final decades of the last century.[2] Strong leadership is all about will and resolve. When there is a tendency to drift, leaders of strength act quickly and resolutely to establish a clear vision and direction. Though aware that some, perhaps many, will suffer as a consequence of "hard decisions," they are ever ready to make those decisions. They are firm and decisive in this way because they are adamant that the "strong" in the society must never be pulled down by the "weak." Against this leadership type, Little identifies the Group Leader. Leaders of this type "are reluctantly aggressive and they idealize solidarity, equality and consultative processes."[3] Further, they are guided in their visioning by social compassion. More recently, we have seen political leaders who are committed to the hardheadedness of economic rationalism at the same time paying at least some attention to the demands of compassion.

It is instructive to contrast these approaches with the kind of leadership God gives in God's engagement with the world. The way God relates to the world is, of course, multifaceted. In relation to suffering

Moving Toward Spiritual Maturity
© 2007 by The Haworth Press, Inc. All rights reserved.
doi:10.1300/5886_07

and injustice, what stands out above all else is the depth of the divine love and mercy. God's heart is overflowing with tenderness as God sets about alleviating the suffering of the weak and the oppressed. It is very clear, then, whose side God takes in the social conflict. There is a reversal of the commitment in the strong leadership approach referred to by Little. Everything gets turned upside down. The "strong leader" aims to ensure that the weak do not drag the strong down. God totally reverses this approach and sides with the poor against the powerful.

> And Yahweh said, "I have seen the miserable state of my people in Egypt. I have heard their appeal to be free of their slave-drivers. Yes, I am well aware of their sufferings. I mean to deliver them out of the hands of the Egyptians. . . ." (Ex 3:7-8)

Wherever there is pain and suffering, whatever the cause, God acts strongly to promote healing and liberation. In love and mercy, God worked a "second Exodus" in the death and resurrection of Jesus to deliver God's people from the slavery of sin. Those of us who share in the life of God's community are called upon to embody God's values and commitments. Unlike the Group Leader who simply finds a place for compassion in her or his agenda, we are to place it at the center of our concerns.

In what follows, the aim is to sketch the outlines of a spirituality of compassion. This will involve exploring the biblical understanding of compassion. Here, we will see that for the biblical writers compassion is a visceral experience, an experience of taking the pain of others into the heart of one's being. In a word, one feels the pain of the other "in the guts." Another way of referring to this experience of solidarity with the hurting person is to use the metaphor of "hospitality." As hosts, we receive the other with her hurts and burdens; we invite her into our personal space. Beyond this personal expression, hospitality in the Christian tradition has the added dimension of community. The individual reaches out in love to others in concert with her sisters and brothers in Christ. In this way, the Christian community becomes a sign of and avenue for God's compassionate welcome in the world. Finally, it is in prayer that we host the troubled and the hurting who are both near and far away. And in prayer, we encounter the One who is able to renew us in our love and compassion, especially when we are feeling overwhelmed by a suffering world. These, then, are the themes to be developed: compassion in the Bible, compassion as hospitality, the compassionate community, and prayer as solidarity. And running through the entire discussion will be the theme of hospitality.

COMPASSION IN THE BIBLE

Dianne Bergant observes that in the cluster of Hebrew words for compassion,[4] *rhm* is the most prominent.[5] It has the primary meaning of "cherishing," "soothing," or "a gentle attitude of mind." It refers to a tender parental love. The word *rehem,* meaning womb, is also derived from this root. Hence, Bergant concludes that this Hebrew word-group indicates a bond like that between a mother and the child of her womb.[6]

Xavier Leon-Dufour describes the Hebrew notion of compassion, as we would expect, in a very similar way. He suggests that *rhm* "expresses the instinctive attachment of one person for another."[7] He observes that this feeling has its seat in the maternal bosom or in the bowels (or, as we would say, heart) of the father. It is a tenderness which drives a person to action on behalf of those in distress.

The New Testament writers often use *éleos* (mercy) when speaking of compassion.[8] A form of the verb *oiktiro* (connoting sympathy) also appears. However, when reference is made to the compassion of Jesus, *splánchnon* is always used. In early Greek usage, the word denotes the "inward parts" of a sacrifice.[9] Later, it was used to refer to the "inward parts of the body," and finally to the womb. We also find the noun form used in the *Testaments of the Twelve Patriarchs.* There it denotes "the center of feelings" or "noble feelings." Once the verb is used to indicate mere emotion, but it generally refers to the inner disposition which generates acts of mercy. The adjective, *eúsplanchnos* (tender-hearted), denotes human virtue and the disposition of "pity."

The noun appears in three of Jesus' parables: the Good Samaritan, the Prodigal Son, and the Unmerciful Servant. Of particular interest for our discussion is the way Paul describes compassion. Only the noun occurs in his writings. He uses *splánchna* not merely to express natural emotions but as "a very forceful term to signify an expression of the total personality at the deepest level."[10] It occurs twice in Philemon (vv. 7, 20); reference is made to the refreshing of the *splánchna*. In verse 12 of that letter, Paul says that in Onesimus he is, in effect, coming in person with a claim for Philemon's love. Phil 1:8 contains a unique phrase. Paul declares that "God can testify how I long for all of you with the affection *(splánchna)* of Jesus Christ." The reference is to "the love or affection which, gripping or moving the whole personality, is possible only in Christ . . ."[11]

In these various uses of the word *compassion* by the biblical authors, there are a number of key features. First, the idea of tenderness comes out in a number of places. Second, compassion is associated with an instinctive, intimate relationship: it is like the loving, soothing action of a mother or father. Last, it refers (most clearly in Pauline usage) not just to an emotion, but to the deepest part of one's personality. This depth dimension is indicated by the cluster of inner parts identifying the seat of the emotion, namely the womb, the bowels, and the heart. We moderns naturally take these organismic references as metaphorical. It seems, however, that the Semite view of emotion was very definitely psychosomatic.

Biblical scholar Terrence Collins has carried out a very careful study of a number of Old Testament references to emotional disturbances and concluded that they are not distinguished from physical disturbances.[12] He describes how the Hebrew person views distressing circumstances as producing a physiological reaction in a person, which starts in his intestines and then proceeds to affect the whole body, especially the heart. This physical disturbance is thought of as actually altering the tone of the organ; there is a general "softening up." Thus, when a person changes his mind or experiences an alteration in his emotional disposition, there is an associated change in the physical composition of the heart.[13] In Hosea 11:8, for example, the change of heart is characterized by strong emotional overtones of compassion, along with the physical reaction connected with "becoming hot." In concluding his investigations, Collins states that the way the Old Testament writers describe the tears associated with both compassion and personal distress is "expressive of a whole anthropology which is essentially psychosomatic, and which allows no distinction between physiological and emotional disturbances. In the biblical view, 'sickness of heart' and 'a broken heart' mean exactly what they say."[14]

This psychosomatic view of emotion, of course, seems odd to us today. We naturally think of the organismic descriptions of emotional reactions in the Old Testament as metaphorical. What these striking somatic references indicate very clearly, nonetheless, is the depth of compassion in the Hebrew people. When a kinsperson was suffering, the empathic reaction was so strong it felt like the very composition of the heart was changing, was "softening up."

In the Bible, then, we have a picture of compassion according to which a person is in such deep solidarity with the pain of another that she takes that pain into herself. She receives the other in her suffering and distress in her inmost space (the heart or the womb). It is, then, as if she hosts the suffering person.

COMPASSION AS HOSPITALITY

Henri Nouwen develops this idea of compassion as hospitality in his book, *The Wounded Healer.*[15] He suggests that a hospitable presence embraces both *concentration* and *community*. If we are to host another and his pain, we must pay attention to him. What stops us from doing this, of course, is our self-preoccupation. Our minds become so full of our own current concerns, random thoughts, and action plans that there is no space left to receive the communications of our guest. Hospitality requires preparing a place, our home, for the one we have invited. If our guest arrives and finds instead of a ready and available space a hive of activity he feels like an intruder. Similarly, to host the wounded one, we must clear away our "intentions," our concerns and desires, and make him feel welcome. "Anyone who wants to pay attention without intention has to be at home in his own house—that is, he has to discover the center of his life in his own heart."[16]

In offering hospitality to a hurting person, there is, says Nouwen, an experience of community. The offering of a compassionate presence is not an offer to take away all pain and suffering. To live, to be mortal, is to live with loneliness, anxiety, and brokenness. Ministry to others is primarily about creating a unity with the other. Because we are there as friend, the other is no longer alone in her loneliness. Because we are there without pretence, anxiety and brokenness can be shared. Because we are there as fellow traveler, we are able to look forward together in hope. Together we search for signs of freedom and new life. "Through this common search, hospitality becomes community. Hospitality becomes community as it creates a unity based on the shared confession of our basic brokenness and on a shared hope."[17]

THE COMPASSIONATE COMMUNITY

The smallest unit of community is two fellow travelers sharing life and hope. In the Christian story, the bond of love becomes stronger, richer, and deeper as it is developed across a network of relationships. "The whole group of believers was united, heart and soul; no one claimed for his own use anything that he had, as everything they owned was held in common" (Acts 4:32). To live in the community of which Christ is the head is to conform oneself to his mind. The way Christ thinks and feels about the world is shaped by love, compassion, and tenderness. In the letter to the Colossians, the author uses the evocative image of "clothing" to indicate complete conformity to the way of Christ. "You are the people of God; he loved you and chose you for his own. So then, you must clothe yourself with compassion, kindness, humility, gentleness, and patience" (Col 3:12). The early Christian community, while it had its own unique expression, was molded and inspired by Israel's corporate life under Yahweh's love and guidance.

Paul Hanson has traced the idea of community throughout the entire Bible.[18] In looking at his discussion, we will see, not unexpectedly, that a central role is accorded to compassion. Hanson suggests that the most fundamental characteristic of the notion of community in the Bible is the way the corporate life of the People of God is based on a pattern of divine initiative and human response.[19] God acts graciously on behalf of the people to secure their freedom and well-being, and they respond in love and fidelity. The shape of their response can be described quite precisely. It has three fundamental elements: worship, righteousness, and *compassion*. Israel became a people because of the divine initiative. Yahweh saw the suffering of the Hebrew slaves and in grace and mercy moved to set them free and to lead them into a land of plenty. The primary response of Israel to God's "antecedent grace" was worship. Together the people praised and glorified the name of the One who delivered them and sustained them. Through their time in the wilderness they came to know Yahweh's abiding care. Yahweh was for them the faithful One, the God of steadfast love *(hesed)*. Without this sustaining love, the people formed in and through the redemptive act would not have survived. Yahweh's *hesed* brought the young community to maturity. In response to all the wonderful deeds of their God, the people joined together in worship.

Through the Torah, the divine instruction, Israel was directed to reflect in its communal life the righteousness *(sedeq)* of Yahweh. In a most comprehensive way, the social, moral, religious, practical, and familial life of the people came under the divine teaching. God instructed the people in the way of justice. While the *Torah* constituted a strict and stringent code, it was softened by a constant reference to love and mercy. "For a community to have a heart, justice had to be infused with compassion."[20] Just as Yahweh shows compassion to all people, and especially the poor, the sojourners, the widows, and orphans, so it must be for those who have covenanted with Yahweh.

As we consider Hanson's treatment of Jesus' interpretation of the community of faith, we will see that his interpretation constituted both confirmation of the experience of Israel and a radically new expression. The Kingdom or Realm of God is, of course, the central theme in Jesus' message. In promoting his understanding of God's Realm, Jesus collided with the beliefs and convictions of the Pharisees. The Pharisaic party propagated a religious system that was the product of centuries of rigorous reflection and careful refinement. Further, they were convinced that the system they were living under and mediating to others had its origins in Yahweh's supreme gift on Mount Sinai, the Torah. According to their interpretation of the Torah, it is only by maintaining a code of ritual purity that they could expect God's blessings to continue. The maintenance of the identity as the People of God required the preservation of purity in their closed fellowship. In a manner that was truly shocking to them, however, Jesus opened fellowship to tax collectors and sinners. Here was Jesus, they thought, destroying the entire concept of religious community; for how is it possible to maintain such a community when the distinction between the holy and the profane is broken down?

Jesus, for his part, was operating out of a radically new and different understanding of God's intention for the community of the faithful and, beyond them, for the whole world. Because he had a sense that the Realm of God was imminent, he believed that membership in the community must be redefined. All concern with ritual purity was irrelevant in this radically different context. Only one criterion applied now, namely, repentance of sin and acceptance of divine grace. Jesus did not destroy the notion of community by casting off all distinctions, but rather "redefined community by removing it from social conventions, and placing it directly within the eschatological context of divine initiative and human response."[21] Though Jesus' understanding of the imminent Reign of God constituted a crucially important innovation in the tradition, we see also that his understanding of God's relationship to the community maintains the centrality of God's gracious initiative and the faithful response of the people. Further, at the heart of the message of Jesus is the notion that everyone, saints and sinners alike, are invited to share in the life of God's Realm. The Son of Man comes as host of a heavenly banquet in which all are invited to share in the love and goodness of God. Moreover, it is especially to the marginalized lot that the compassionate heart of God is opened. At the table, Jesus sits down with tax collectors and sinners.

It is the vocation of the community of faith to reach out in compassion to others, especially those shunted to the sidelines of societal life. Just before the turn of this century, I spent three years in Edinburgh, Scotland. While I was there, I reconnected with my good friend, Douglas Galbraith. During one of our conversations, Douglas referred to his experience as part of the ministry team in the Craigmillar Parish of the Church of Scotland. The way in which the Parish folk connected with the community around them is quite remarkable. Douglas tells the story in *Music in the Listening Place*.[22]

At the time of Douglas' involvement, and to date, the Craigmillar community was one struggling with a variety of social problems. It was viewed by many as an area for "dropouts." Here were people heavily dependent on handouts and professional assistance. Indeed, the leading Edinburgh newspaper, *The Scotsman*, ran a headline on Craigmillar that read, "Estate with Its Own Psychiatrist." But Douglas identifies another way of viewing this battling inner-city area. The outline of this image, though not immediately obvious, is "that of a viable community which was beginning to influence and shape the lives of those who lived in it."[23] In offering support for the project of building up its communal life, the Craigmillar Parish made a number of responses. But the most significant contribution took two forms: music making and hospitality.

You may be wondering how music could play a significant role in the life of a struggling inner-city community. The music offered by the Parish was not the music of entertainment but rather the music of protest. Protest would become necessary in response to a new traffic plan. Edinburgh is of course a very old city and totally unprepared for the demands of modern transportation. There is a pressing need to relieve inner-city traffic. As part of a plan to respond to this need, a new ring road was proposed. While it would relieve inner-city traffic, it would also have a devastating effect on the attempt to bring the Craigmillar community together. The new road would, in fact, chop the community in half. Those in the decision-making process, observing that most of the residents were living in accommodation rented from the local authority, were of the view that the people of Craigmillar were unlikely to have any real pride in their community. It was assumed that most of the residents would worry little about the destructive impact of a new road system. But they were wrong. Through the Craigmillar Festival, the local folk made their musical protest and they showed that they cared and that the unity and integrity of their community was vitally important to them. Douglas, a very talented musician, responded to a request from the Craigmillar folk to take on the key role of musical director for the festival. Apart from allowing him to contribute his gifts, his involvement provided him with an avenue for listening. "[H]ere was an opportunity to put one's ear to the ground," he reflects, "to listen and learn, to hear about what was valued, what was visioned, in a more subtle way than a survey could offer."[24]

Indeed, the challenge for the Parish community as a whole was to learn how to listen with openness and understanding. Perhaps, not surprisingly, the relationship between the two communities was not always so strong and positive. The Parish folk had to learn to correct their distorted images and understandings of the surrounding community. At first, they did not listen at all, but rather went their own way, offering to the people around them what they thought was needed. In a move to renovate church life, the leadership team developed an exciting new program of worship, Christian education, and outreach. But within the local community these activities presented as largely irrelevant. The parish people learned the valuable, and of course quite painful, lesson that it is only through dialogue that people connect with one another.

> What was required . . . was not more explanations, fresh words, more telling programmes. We needed to still the monologue and re-create the silence into which the Word first took form, so that it might find expression again in this community without static and interference from either side obscuring its clarity.[25]

In and through the dialogue, the real needs of the community emerged. The Craigmillar folk asked for, as I have already indicated, a composer and musical director to help them shape their protest; they made a request for space to host various community activities; and they identified the need for a meeting place providing low-cost refreshments. In response to the latter two requests, the church property was made available, and a café was opened on the premises. The Craigmillar Parish set about, then, creating a hospitable space for the local people.

Hospitality begins with dialogue. If there is no listening place, a caring act, although well-meant, can be misguided and ultimately irrelevant. The Christian community has the vocation of inviting others into that space permeated with the love, grace, and peace of God. To think that we *create* this space is a common distraction and delusion. We don't so much create it as find it. As the experience of the Craigmillar Parish demonstrates so powerfully, finding the way of compassion begins with "stilling" the monologue and listening in the silence.

PRAYER AS SOLIDARITY

Along with the physical provision of hospitality, there is another way in which we can host others who are suffering. In prayer, we invite others, with their burdens and distresses, into that inmost place where God is present in love and mercy. It may seem that to host others through prayer is to retreat from the real demands of compassion. It may seem like compassion in a world of virtual reality: we approach the pain and suffering of others through imagination and mental processes. But in fact, as Nouwen et al. point out, prayer is "the first expression of human solidarity."[26] Prayer is an act of solidarity with the suffering ones

> [b]ecause the Spirit who prays in us is the Spirit by whom all human beings are brought together in unity and community. The Holy Spirit, the Spirit of peace, unity, and reconciliation, constantly reveals himself to us as the power through whom people from the most diverse social, political, economic, racial, and ethnic backgrounds are brought together as sisters and brothers of the same Christ and daughters and sons of the same Father.[27]

Now of course, as Nouwen et al. are well aware, such language can easily take us into romanticism and sentimentality. The fact is that to be physically present is much more demanding and costly than to connect with others spiritually. What is vitally important, then, is that we open ourselves to the Spirit and to the claim that she is making on our lives. The Spirit is calling us to responsibility. It is not that we are asked to respond to each and every need; such a thought is patently ridiculous. What is required of us is a sensitive and open listening to God as we are directed to those people, issues, and situations requiring our active compassionate response. If we cannot feel the pull of the Spirit in this way, our talk of prayer as "the first expression of human solidarity" will be very hollow indeed.

I do not wish, however, to diminish the importance of the notion of spiritually hosting others in their suffering. In this modern era of mass communication, the rest of the world has come very close to us. It is just twelve inches away as I read my newspaper or magazine. It is right there in my lounge room as I turn on the television. The agonies and anguish of our sisters and brothers in the world community sit right under our noses. But of course, the great pain of the world is also thousands of miles away. We can't reach out with a physical touch of love and tenderness. Prayer, though, offers us a very real way in which we can be in solidarity with the suffering of those who are at a distance. As we pray, we can establish an empathic connection with them. In the presence of the compassionate Spirit of Christ, we are able to think and feel our way into their experience. We invite them into our inmost center. "To pray for others means to make them part of ourselves. To pray for others means to allow their pains and sufferings, their anxieties and loneliness, their confusion and fears to resound in our innermost selves."[28]

Compassionate prayer is not only, though, about reaching out to the unknown ones far away and the loved ones near at hand. We are also required to pray with compassion for those who have injured and wronged us. More specifically, we are to pray for those people for whom we feel little or no love. We are asked to invite into our inmost space those people whom we desperately want to keep at a distance, our enemies. "You have learnt," Jesus teaches, "how it was said: You must love your neighbor and hate your enemy. But I say to you: love your enemies and pray for those who persecute you . . ." (Mt 5:43-45). Is there a more challenging teaching in the gospels?

Gary was a lay leader in a former congregation. He was a man who had to have his own way. If he felt he was losing ground in a church council meeting, he would resort to bullying to advance his cause. The strategy was a successful one. Others had different views, but were afraid to cross Gary. Those of us who dared to promote alternative visions became his sworn enemies. After being on the wrong end of a number of "tongue-lashings" from Gary, a strong dislike for him developed in me. Well, actually, I probably should confess that I hated him. For a very long time, I could not bear to bring his name before God. To do so, I thought, would be like defiling a sacred place. When I eventually did, something quite profound happened. I would like to be able to say that I suddenly felt compassion for my adversary. But, instead, I experienced a different kind of change. For the first time, I began to see my own failings in the encounters I had with Gary. Despite a couple of frank conversations with him in which I attempted to help him see the destructive dimension in his way of relating to others, there was no conversion experience for Gary. To his credit, he certainly made efforts to change, but he very quickly slid back into his old ways. Perhaps I wasn't able to help Gary, but he helped me. Or rather, in praying about his faults, I became more acutely aware of my own. I became aware that my fear and dislike of confrontation meant that I let some things go that I shouldn't have. In this way, I failed both him and the other members of our faith community.

SUMMARY

Compassion is an experience in which the suffering of the other is received in one's inmost self. It is, then, an act of hospitality. We as individual Christians may feel overwhelmed by the task of hosting the depth and breadth of pain and distress that we encounter. But we are not asked to be lone bearers of compassion in the world. The Christian story is one of a community of love and care reaching out to others. In community we are able to much more effectively radiate the world with God's compassionate love. While we cannot always connect physically with the suffering ones in the world, in prayer we have the opportunity to meet them spiritually. Prayer is an expression of solidarity with those who are hurting and burdened. The greatest challenge we face is to enter into solidarity with those who have hurt us. Compassion is to be extended not only to those we like, but also to our enemies.

PART IV:
CONSCIENCE AND RESPONSIBILITY

Chapter 8

Conscience
and "Contrast Experiences"

In this final section, we open a window into the moral sphere. The theme running through our reflections here is *responsibility*. To act in a responsible manner means to be accountable for our decisions and actions, and to be responsive to the claims of others.

Responsibility and conscience are closely connected. In this chapter, we give attention to the role of the inner voice in keeping us oriented to God's good purposes. But what do we mean by conscience, exactly? It is sometimes referred to as that inner forum in which a person gets in touch with her highest moral values. As she reflects honestly and openly in her inner center, she subjects both past and future events to her best moral judgments. She forms her best judgment about the rightness or wrongness in past actions and events, and she is able to make a decision as to what would constitute the good in future actions and events. Importantly, she is not alone in this inner forum. It is not just her own voice that she listens to, but many others as well. For a Christian, the most significant contributing voice is that of the Spirit of Christ. The Spirit's voice is most often heard as the voice behind many other voices. The conscience is informed by input from a variety of sources. As we turn to the scriptures, Abraham and Moses, Ruth and Esther, Paul, and John and, of course, Jesus himself, all speak to us about what is right and good in God's eyes. The other great moral guides in the Christian tradition join with this band. Last, contemporary men and women of moral wisdom make their contribution to the debate that goes on in the inner forum. So in listening to

Moving Toward Spiritual Maturity
© 2007 by The Haworth Press, Inc. All rights reserved.
doi:10.1300/5886_08

the inner voice, we are really listening for the voice of God. But God uses many voices to give shape to God's guidance.

For quite some time now, the role of conscience has been looked upon by many with caution, and by some with deep suspicion. It seems safe to say that a major reason for this is the fact that Freud's notion of the superego has taken root in our consciousness. The superego is often experienced as a negative conscience. It represents the control exerted on a person by a range of external authorities. The rules and prohibitions of parents, teachers, and other authority figures become internalized and shape the responses that a person makes in her engagements in the world. This is not an altogether bad thing, of course. Some of the rules that are internalized are part of the social consensus concerning what constitutes the good and are therefore valuable to have as part of one's moral code. Moreover, it is useful if one does not have to constantly reflect on what is appropriate in any given situation, but can sometimes act automatically instead. What is negative in the functioning of the superego, however, is that guilt becomes a weapon used against personal freedom and autonomy. That is, a person, fearful of the guilt feelings she will have if she does not follow the internalized rules, acts contrary to her own preferences. Put simply, she lives under the power of "shoulds" and "oughts." With this awareness of the negative impact of the superego, there are those who are either deeply suspicious of the role of conscience, or who dismiss it outright. Clearly, it will be important for us to distinguish a positive conscience from this negative one. In short, the positive conscience that we will be referring to is constituted by an aspiration to central (or key) personal values and ideals. That is, rather than being pushed by externally formed rules, a person experiences a pull to those values and convictions that have been formed internally. She has thought carefully about the values that she believes are important, and she freely and willingly sets about living them out.

One way of talking about this internal set of values and convictions is to refer to a moral vision. Vision has become an important category for some theological ethicists—Stanley Hauerwas being one of the most prominent. His argument is that vision rather than decision is primary in the moral life. We will explore this notion. Further, we will construe conscience as the pull toward one's moral vision.

We have, then, a vision of the way interpersonal, societal, and international relationships should be ordered. That vision is shaped by the central Christian principles of love, compassion, justice, peace, and reconciliation. From time to time, however, we encounter situations that run counter to this vision. We collide with what are sometimes called "contrast experiences." These are experiences that contrast with our moral vision of the way human life should be ordered. Faced with the contrast, our conscience will direct us to take some action to improve the situation. We will spend some time reflecting on how contrast experiences form us for service in the world.

These, then, are the important issues to be discussed: the difference between a negative and a positive conscience, the role of vision in the operation of conscience, and the relationship between conscience and contrast experiences. But let me first say more about what the conscience actually is.

DEFINING CONSCIENCE

Richard Gula helpfully observes that conscience can be viewed in three distinct but interrelated ways: as a *capacity,* as a *process,* and as a *judgment.*[1] The conscience, first, can be viewed as a fundamental capacity to discern good and evil. Apart from those who are severely brain-damaged or emotionally traumatized, everyone is capable, at least in a basic way, of deciding what is right and what is wrong. In order to reach this point of decision, a person engages in a process. She must make use of the moral information that she has at her disposal to decide what makes a good person and what in a given situation constitutes a good and right action. The end result of the process of reflection and analysis is a moral judgment. Having used her personal experience and the moral wisdom of others, she has thought through a number of different scenarios. Finally, she has chosen one of these to enact. Assuming that she has engaged in the process fully and honestly, it represents the best moral option for her.

Positive and Negative Conscience

For some, however, the question would be whether she has really chosen to act in this particular way, or whether her decision has been forced on her by internalized authorities. Informed by Freud's notion of the superego, these persons are concerned that to speak about conscience is really another way of speaking about the tyrannical hold the rules and dictates others have over us.[2] Recall (from Chapter 2) that in the Freudian interpretation of the personality, there are three basic structures: the id, the ego, and the superego. The id is an unconscious store of instinctual drives of both a sexual and an aggressive nature. Under the push of the id, persons experience impulses aimed at experiencing pleasure and at expressing hostility. The ego is the (largely) conscious dimension of the personality. It has the role of mediating the demands of the id, the interpersonal and the physical environments, and more widely, the society and the culture. The superego, as the name suggests, represents the ego of another superimposed on one's own. Using guilt as a powerful means of control, it serves as an internal censor. The superego represents the place where all the "should" and "have to" messages we were bombarded with in the home, in the school, and out in the community are stored. As soon as we find ourselves choosing an action contrary to these messages, we suffer from guilt feelings. The superego tells us that we are good when we follow the rules of the external authorities, and it tells us that we are bad and makes us feel guilty when we deviate from them.

To understand what the superego is and to appreciate how it develops, it is necessary to reflect on our childhood experience. What is of prime value and importance for most, if not all, of us in growing up is the approval and affection of those we love and admire. It is important to us to learn the rules of good and acceptable conduct because we want to know what is going to win approval. To experience the warm glow of parental and social affirmation is a cherished aim. With this state of affairs in view, it is easy to see how the rules, preferences, and prohibitions of authority figures become internalized and continue to exert a strong force long after the childhood years have passed.

While many of the rules and values we pick up in childhood represent a societal moral consensus—"be honest," "care for the needy," "pursue justice," for example—and are extremely worthwhile, others are not worthy of continued allegiance. If we continue to be bound by rules and preferences that we now judge are morally inadequate, we forfeit our freedom and cannot reach a state of moral maturity. Establishing our freedom as morally mature persons involves acting according to our conscience and against the superego. Or to be more specific, it involves acting against those superego dictates that we are convinced are unworthy of our commitment. "[W]e give our lives meaning," writes Richard Gula, "by committing our freedom. The morally mature adult is called to commit his or her freedom, not to submit it. As long as we do not direct our own activity, we are not yet free, morally mature persons."[3]

Let's at this point attempt to identify one or two scenarios in which the impact of the interplay between the superego and the mature conscience might be felt. It may be, for example, that you are feeling prompted to incorporate a sociopolitical dimension into your discipleship. As a result of your reading of the relevant parts of the scriptures and of consulting the moral wisdom of Christian writers and of personal friends, you are feeling convicted that it would be wrong to continue to ignore this area of discipleship. But as you begin to explore ways of making your decision concrete, you find yourself feeling quite uncomfortable. It may be, for instance, that you are joining in your first protest rally. You find yourself feeling distinctly guilty. Now where, we need to ask, are these guilt feelings coming from? You are being assaulted by superego voices: "Introducing politics degrades religion." "Radical views are bad; conservative views are good." "A social gospel is a distortion of the gospel." You are feeling guilty because you feel as though you have betrayed those people who were so significant in your early years, and perhaps continue to be significant. In following the dictates of your conscience, you are asserting your personal freedom and establishing your moral maturity. But not without paying for it.

Here is another scenario. A member of your worship planning team is acting inappropriately. He is tending to dominate and control the team meetings. Speaking frequently and in an overbearing way, he attempts to promote his own views without giving due recognition to the views and the feelings of others. You arrange a private meeting with him to discuss your concerns. During the meeting, you find yourself speaking quite firmly and directly. Your conscience tells you that you have to take action for the sake of the group. You know that it is not going to be pleasant, but you decide to do it anyway. Despite an awareness that you are acting in a morally appropriate way, there is nevertheless a feeling of "wrongness" that is plaguing you. If you tune in, you will hear the superego messages playing: "We must always be nice." "It's bad to make others feel uncomfortable." "Confrontation is undesirable." Again, the path to moral maturity is impeded by superego rules and taboos. Anyone who has had to do battle with these internalized moral voices knows how painful and costly such a battle is. But it is a battle that must be won. Rather than being controlled by outdated, morally inadequate internal messages, we must live in the freedom of our contemporary moral vision.

CONSCIENCE AND VISION

I have used the term "vision" here quite deliberately. While the operation of the conscience involves decision, choice, and action, it may be that vision is even more important. Certainly this is the argument of Stanley Hauerwas. He suggests,

> The moral life is not first a life of choice—decision is not king—but is rather woven from the notions that we use to see and from the situations we confront. Moral life involves learning to see the world through an imaginative ordering of our basic symbols and notions.[4]

Hauerwas argues that Christian ethics has allowed itself to be shaped by the dominant philosophical view of the human as actor and self-creator. According to this view, the human constructs herself through a "willful" actualization of the choices and decisions that she has made. A person decides on the significant actions and plans that will give the desired shape to her life and engages her will to ensure that these are realized. In following Gula in characterizing conscience in terms of judgment, are we not falling in with this model? Well, to an extent we are. But as Hauerwas readily acknowledges, there must be a place for decision in ethical theory and practice. He does not deny the importance of decision and action in the moral life, but rather argues that decisions and actions must be based on a vision of what is most real, meaningful, and worthwhile.[5] When we assess the quality in the moral life of others, we do not look only to the choices they make and the decisions they enact. Rather, we look to something that is much more difficult to grasp but which is also more important, namely, a "total vision of life."[6] This total vision is shown in their way of speaking and relating, in their assessments of others, in the way they think about their own lives and of the world around them, and in what they judge to be noble and of worth. What we are grasping for here is a total way of viewing self, others, life, and God that informs and molds all our words and actions.

As we see, so shall we be. Conscience can be understood as an impetus to live true to one's total vision of life. How, we need to ask, is this vision shaped? In ultimate terms, God is at work in us through the Holy Spirit in shaping the vision. What God requires in order to mold within us a vision that is real, strong, and worthy are two assets. The first is *quality input,* and the second is *quality interpretation.* If we are to see ourselves, others, and God in a way that is real and meaningful, we need to be accessing wise and mature perspectives on the moral life. The kind of reading we do, the way we engage with the scriptures, and the range of persons we interact with, all impact significantly on the moral vision that is forming within us. In a spirit of gratitude, we can see these inputs as personal gifts. Others have gifted us through their words, thoughts, and personhood with a quality vision of life. But we cannot take over their vision directly. We need to interpret their ideas, preferences, values, and actions in order to appropriate them. Contact with excellent input is no guarantee that an excellent vision will form within us. If we fail to fully understand what we are seeing and hearing, our vision suffers. It is the excellence of our interpretation that allows us to shape a worthy vision.

CONSCIENCE AND LIVING A VISION FOR DISCIPLESHIP

The conscience can be viewed as an impetus to remain true to this vision that God is shaping within us. As we look to the local community in which we live and serve, we see a number of challenges. There are issues and concerns that demand a response. But we know that to become involved will be demanding and costly. It is not easy, first, to interpret exactly what is going on in the community. We must deal with the untidiness, confusion, and struggle associated with such an interpretation. Having begun to formulate with some degree of clarity what the issues are, it becomes even more difficult when we attempt to construct an action plan. However, having worked up with others a plan of action, we must deal with the possibility of failure. There is no way ahead of time of knowing how effective our initiative will be. Actualizing new expressions of ministry and mission is an inherently risky enterprise. It would be so much easier to ignore the pressing issues and concerns present in the community and restrict ourselves to established—and therefore safe—Christian practices. Whether or not we will choose the easy path depends on our personal vision. How do we see ourselves as disciple? What are the symbols and metaphors around which that vision is structured? Is it a vision grounded in courage, risk, and fidelity? Or is it molded around safety, predictability, and personal ease?

Let us think more concretely about these community issues. What are some of the issues and concerns that arise for local communities? Well, for some communities homelessness is a serious concern. For others, the plans of developers and/or local government raise significant concerns about environmental degradation. A lack of facilities, finally, in which local youths may meet and recreate is a problem that looms large in some local communities. To encounter these situations is to engage with what some call a "contrast experience."[7] The situation, marked as it is by injustice and suffering, stands in contrast to the biblical vision of shalom. To live in shalom is to live in peace, justice, unity, and well-being. According to C. Platinga, the sin and evil that are all too prevalent constitute a "vandalism of shalom."[8] When we encounter this vandalism, there is a pull to become involved. We become acutely aware that the situation is far from the way it ought to be. It is not God's intention that people should live in deprivation, suffering, and oppression. It is not God's intention that the beautiful world God has created should be deformed and degraded. Where there is injustice and suffering, God is at work to bring liberation. The leading Hebrew Scriptures' paradigm of the divine intention is found in the Book of Exodus:

> Then the Lord said, "I have seen how cruelly my people are being treated in Egypt; I have heard them cry out to be rescued from their slavedrivers. I know all about their sufferings, and so I have come down to rescue them from the Egyptians and to bring them out of Egypt to a spacious land, one which is rich and fertile. . . ." (3:7-8)

Where there is injustice and suffering, God acts to set the captives free. The oppressors, those who are driven by greed and a desire for power and prestige, are also in bondage. Though they may not be aware of it, they are bound in a state of sin. All of us in various ways are the bondslaves of sin. God worked out a "second Exodus" in Christ to set us free from the power of sin and death. God's intention in and through Christ was to establish right relationships in the world. In interpersonal relationships, in international relationships, in the relationship between humans and the earth, and, finally, in the relationship between humans and God, God was at work in Christ bringing reconciliation. Where there are distortions in relationships, where there is pain, abuse, aggression, and injustice, there we encounter a contrast with God's intention.

In a "contrast experience," the conscience is stimulated. We know that this is not the way life and relationships ought to be. There is a deep awareness that something ought to be done to improve the situation. Perhaps we hear the voice of conscience: "You need to take some action in this situation."

Now it is clearly not possible to respond in every context of contrast. To personally take on too many battles is also something that contrasts with the divine intention. When we overcommit ourselves, our emotional and physical well-being is placed in jeopardy, as are our relationships with friends and family members. In any case, spreading one's social action too thinly is simply not effective. Tom Malone's practical approach to establishing priorities is instructive. He recommends asking the question: "[O]f all these struggles, which has the least money, the fewest supporters, and the greatest risk from lack of public advocacy?"[9] This is clearly a useful strategy. I want to suggest, moreover, that the inner light of the Spirit guides us in this kind of decision making. There will be those occasions in which we feel a very strong pull to become involved. It will become clear that this is an issue that simply cannot be left to others. The leading of the Holy Spirit seems insistent. To make a contribution is something that she is asking of us. It may or may not be the case, I hasten to add, that the cause in question fits the criteria that Malone establishes.

There is also, of course, the question of the level of response. It is often not simply a matter of getting involved or not getting involved. In working for change, there are various levels of engagement. At one end of the spectrum, there are low-level activities such as communicating a protest and a proposal for change through letters, faxes, e-mail, petitions, or through joining in marches and rallies. Joining an activist group and participating in its protests takes a person to the upper end of the involvement spectrum. To take on leadership of such a group places one in the category of very high engagement. Conscience is a guide to the level of involvement that is right for us personally. If we are avoiding the option of a significant level of engagement in a particular issue and often feel disturbed in our spirit, it may well be that we are failing to respond to the voice of conscience.

This issue of the level of our engagement points us to the general question of weighing up one's own private welfare over against the public good. As I have just indicated, it is in the inner forum that this question needs to be settled. But this inner court can only do its work properly when it receives input from wise and truthful sources. One very significant source in relation to the issue at hand is Dr. Martin Luther King Jr. He reminds us that our focus needs to be on the plight of the oppressed rather than on our own needs, anxieties, and concerns. The following message was spoken on the night before he was murdered in Memphis.

> That's the question before you tonight. Not, "If I stop to help the sanitation workers, what will happen to all of the hours that I usually spend in my office every day and every week as a pastor?" The question is not, "If I stop to help this man in need, what will happen to me?" "If I do not stop to help the sanitation workers, what will happen to them?" That's the question.[10]

SUMMARY

We began by describing conscience in terms of a capacity, a process, and a judgment. In the absence of mitigating circumstances, a person has a capacity to discern good and evil. In order to decide how she should act, she enters into a process of moral analysis and reflection. The end result of this process is a concrete judgment concerning action.

What is important in this process is that a person is guided by values and preferences she personally owns. The alternative is to be pushed by values and preferences of others that have been uncritically internalized. To be pushed in this way is to be caught in the grip of superego commands. The aim is to live out of a mature conscience and so to reach for the ideals that one has freely chosen.

The set of values and ideals that shape our moral life constitutes our total vision of life. Although, as we have seen, judgment and decision are important in the exercise of conscience, ultimately these activities are grounded in personal vision. A crucial question for the Christian, then, is this: What is my vision of myself as person and as disciple? This question cannot be asked in isolation from these questions: How do I view other people? The society? The earth? God?

From time to time we encounter situations in which there is a contrast with our personal vision. This personal vision should be grounded in the Christian vision of shalom in the world. In these situations, conscience may spur us to work for change. We cannot respond significantly in every context of contrast. Here again the voice of conscience plays an important role. It is this voice that tells us which issues we simply cannot ignore.

Chapter 9

The Agape Response

At the end of Chapter 8, we were deeply challenged by Dr. Martin Luther King Jr.'s exhortation to look first to the needs of the oppressed rather than to our own. In a word, he was calling for an agape response. Agape love involves giving of one's self for the sake of the other.

Back in Chapter 1, we saw that Gary Badcock suggests that cross-bearing—self-giving in the service of others—is at the heart of the Christian vocation. Cross-bearing is only possible when we are infused with agape. Many would want to say that the whole meaning of the Christian ethic is summed up in this sentence. There is clearly strong biblical support for placing agape right at the center of discipleship. In the gospels we find repeated exhortations to deny self for the sake of one's neighbor. But it is unhelpful, I contend, to challenge the disciples of Christ with self-giving without also including a strong statement on the importance of self-love. Self-giving and self-love need to be in balance in the way we live out our commitment to Christ.

I will attempt to show that selflessness is an inadequate moral and spiritual goal for those of us engaged in mounting a Christian response to the needs of the world. In order to do this, I will present statements by moral theologians on the relationship between self-love and other-love that I believe are more helpful than a one-sided affirmation of the centrality of cross-bearing. Gene Outka, first, has argued for the notion of "universal love." With this concept, he attempts to take seriously the demands of both love for self and love for neighbor. Stephen Post is another moral theologian who attempts to pay due regard to the importance of self-love. He identifies the ideal

Moving Toward Spiritual Maturity
© 2007 by The Haworth Press, Inc. All rights reserved.
doi:10.1300/5886_09

of Christian love as "communion." That is, fulfillment is found not in selflessness but in a relationship of giving and receiving. But first, let me say more about what constitutes the agape response.

AGAPE

Agape is self-giving for the sake of the other. Jesus teaches us to turn the other cheek, to walk the extra mile, and to love our enemies. Gene Outka's term for this kind of love is "equal regard."[1] Friend or enemy, intelligent or dull, attractive or not—everyone is deserving of our respect, consideration, and care. Anders Nygren, in his classic treatise on agape, refers time and again to the fact that it is sovereign and not dependent, spontaneous and not motivated.[2] We who are agapists are not compelled to love; we choose to love. We are not driven by the thought of personal gain; we are moved by the love of God channeling through us.

All of us find it easy to love those that we experience as attractive. Agapists find a way to love the unlovable. They may not feel like loving, but they have a strong enough will to make it happen. Edward Vacek agrees that will plays a central role in expressing agape. But he does not want to take the idea that love transcends negative feelings to mean that emotion is unimportant. "When our action originates in emotion, we are more fully engaged in our acts and not simply 'going through the motions.' We love only when we have been *moved* and *attracted* to affirm the beloved's (real and ideal) goodness."[3] Giving of the self for the other does not come easily to us; we therefore need to engage the will. But if we act strictly out of a sense of duty, purely on the strength of personal volition, our good works lose some of their goodness. No one wants to feel like an object of pity. Genuine love requires a personal engagement with the other.

OUTKA AND "UNIVERSAL LOVE"

Outka begins his highly detailed analysis[4] of Christian love by suggesting that a good general principle to start with is impartiality or "equal regard." This principle indicates the way in which we should love others, but it should also be applied to self-love. The notion that every other person is to be loved simply because he or she is a child of

God should operate in my relationship with myself. Others are neither more nor less deserving of my love than I am. I should regard others and myself equally.

Outka develops his argument in this way. Christians are called to love others. We are called to love not only those who are likable, or who have done something good for us, but *all* people. Loving only our "favorites" is not an option. We must love each and every person God puts in our path. The theological rationale is based around our status as children of God. Each and every person is created in the image of God. He or she is someone Christ died for. It follows that each and every person possesses an inherent dignity and worth. Just as God recognizes that value through the gift of divine love, so it is to be with us. God does not have favorites, and neither should we. This leads Outka to refer to the principle of "impartiality." It is clear that we are to love others simply because of their status in God's eyes: a person created out of love and offered the loving gift of Christ on the cross. We need, says Outka, to apply the same theological rationale to ourselves. We are to love the self for the same reason that we love others. There is therefore a principle of "equal regard." We should love the self neither more nor less than we love others.

Don Browning has taken up Outka's suggestion and developed it in a number of contexts.[5] He helpfully points out that the principle of equal regard constitutes a middle way between the extremes of independence, on the one hand, and self-sacrifice, on the other. In the independence or self-actualization model of love, it is assumed that self-love comes first, and that love of neighbor will follow automatically. That is, the focus is largely on self-fulfillment and the extent to which a particular act or relationship is likely to contribute to it. At the other end of the scale is an understanding of love that requires sacrificing the self for others. The equal regard approach, Browning suggests, picks up values from the other two models, but it manages to avoid their excesses. A person living according to the principle of equal regard will take the needs and claims of the other as seriously as her own. The needs of others are seen to be very important, but so are one's own. Love for others and self-love are assigned an equal weighting.

While the equal regard model constitutes a good starting point, Outka argues that we should go a step further and talk about what he calls "universal love."[6] Though it is closely associated with impartiality, it also moves beyond it to incorporate the Christian commitment to being for the other. (Here, let me point out, he is acknowledging the importance of cross-bearing.) Let me also point out that though he does not use the term "universal love," Browning is clearly aware of the importance of the principle. "Self-sacrifice and the demands of the cross," he writes, "are still required in this love ethic. Sometimes we must love even when circumstances do not permit us to be loved fully in return."[7]

Outka lists four challenges to the principle of impartiality.[8] It is the first two that are particularly relevant to our discussion. They are these. First, impartiality cannot find a place for the radically other-regarding elements in agape. Second, it does not take seriously the fact that we are more likely to be tempted by selfishness than by altruism. Outka is prepared to align himself with impartiality to the extent that altruism is not given endorsement if it is of the radical kind that is dismissive of self-love. However, in taking these two objections seriously, he suggests that it is necessary to go beyond impartiality and incorporate "a practical swerve" away from self and toward the other.[9] Given the fact that virtually everyone has great difficulty in being even-handed when it comes to balancing personal needs against those of the other person, it is necessary to build in a bias toward the well-being of the other.

Outka's proposal is attractive because it acknowledges that the needs of the self do matter, while offering a way to counteract the almost universal temptation to selfishness that mitigates other-regard. What is lacking in Outka's analysis, however, is recognition of the prime importance of mutuality or communion in the ethics of love. He certainly acknowledges very clearly that the needs of the self are important and must be attended to, but he does not go further and identify communion as a crucial need of the self. This is where Stephen Post's work is most helpful.

POST AND "COMMUNION"

According to Post, mutual love or reciprocity is the only appropriate basic norm for interpersonal relations.[10] He also refers to this mutual love as "communion." He argues that there is a "true" self-love that is expressed through a desire for a triadic fellowship involving God, self, and other(s).[11] One pursues one's own needs and aspirations, but only in the context of a loving commitment to the needs and aspirations of those with whom one shares life. Such a reciprocal love, argues Post, is not inferior to selfless love, as many believe:

> The moral excellence of communion (giving and receiving love) is too often lost sight of . . . Frequently selfless love . . . is thought to be ethically superior to communion and alone worthy of the designation "Christian." The equilibrium of communion that allows each participant to find fulfillment through the process of mutuality is set aside to make room for the rare genius of selflessness. However, in our view, a "true" or proper self-love defined as the pursuit of one's own good within the context of triadic communion can be distinguished from both selfishness (the pursuit of one's own separate interests) and self-infatuation.[12]

Post argues, then, that it is legitimate to pursue one's own good within the context of a triadic fellowship. Such self-love must be distinguished from both selfishness and self-infatuation. Selfishness means pursuing one's own interests without due regard for the interests of others. But when one is committed to a life of communion, one pays due attention to the needs and desires of others. A person who is self-infatuated, on the other hand, simply cannot manage fellowship with others. She is so attracted to self that she finds no interest in getting to know others in any depth. The good of personal fulfillment, by contrast, is pursued through a relationship of reciprocity. One desires fulfillment for oneself, but one is equally concerned with helping others find it.

Post's basic argument is that the ideal of a love stripped of all self-concern is grounded in a mistaken conceptualization of divine love. Self-concern, it is important to recognize, is very different from selfishness. There are legitimate concerns that the self has and these need to be taken care of. A central concern that God has is the mutual good of communion with human persons.

Post turns to both the Hebrew and the Christian scriptures to demonstrate that God is not disinterested in the way God loves humankind. In the Bible we find a picture of a God who grieves. Yahweh "was sorry that he made humanity on earth," we read in Genesis, "and he was grieved at heart" (6:6). Why is God grieved? Because God reaches out in love calling humanity into communion, and time and again people reject that call. If God's love were disinterested, this grieving would make no sense. But if we take God's deep concern for the mutual good of fellowship seriously, we also give due credit to the important human vocation of soothing divine pain through promoting that fellowship.

Post uses Abraham Heschel's discussion in *Between God and Man* to discuss this vocation. The Israelite prophets, says Heschel, had as their goal the mitigation of the divine *pathos* that is associated with rejection by humans. In calling the people to turn away from their sin in order to turn anew to God and to the divine will and purpose, they were attempting to change God's pathos into joy. According to Heschel, it is simply not possible to find the ideal of selfless love in the Hebrew scriptures. What we find, instead, is a profound valuation of a reciprocal relationship of love between God and humanity. Communion between Yahweh and Israel is the vision, the desideratum, the ultimate aim as far as the writers of the Hebrew scriptures are concerned. Certainly there is no place for an egocentricity that places the "I" at the center of the universe. But self-concern is quite distinct from selfishness. A passionate concern for the mutual good of fellowship is not only legitimate, it should be vigorously pursued. "Mutuality, not mere giving, is the goal of love."[13] Yahweh gives fully of the divine self, but Yahweh also desires a response of love. The Hebrew Bible reveals a God "on the make," if you will.

Heschel, Post notes, amasses a vast array of scriptural references to support this contention. Here are just a few of his examples: "You hunt me like a lion" (Jb 10:16); "The voice of the Lord cries to the city" (Mi 6:9); and finally, the Lord calls out, "Where are you?" (Gn 3:9). All of these texts point to the fact that God is unwilling to be alone and pursues humans in the hope of establishing fellowship with them.

We have established that God's love for us is not disinterested, but what about the call to imitate Christ? Surely he is the model of a life totally devoid of self-interest and self-love. Post argues that while the Christ of the gospels is never selfish, it is misleading to suggest that he has no self-concern. The concern Jesus has is the same as that of the Father: to call humans into communion. Once this goal was lost and those who valued power and privilege more than fellowship with God began to exert their influence, the way of the cross was established as the way of salvation. God's hope in Christ was for everyone to hear the message of the Realm of God and to respond. The fact that certain powerful ones did not and moved so viciously against Jesus meant that God's saving love, originally channeled through Jesus' healing and preaching ministry, would now be focused on the cross.

Does it follow that the cross is now established as the ultimate goal of all love? If so, it has to be admitted that self-sacrifice rather than mutuality is the final aim of love. Post contends that it is not necessary to go down this path. Following Richard Westley, he takes the view that the cross is only one dimension in the salvation event:

> [T]he deepest desire of [Jesus'] heart was that people would respond to his proclamation and have a change of heart. But if he knew that the human race could only be saved on the condition of his own bloody murder, then he could not want "everyone" to be transformed by his message. If everyone responded . . . there would be none left to administer his violent death. To hold that it was only through his passion and death on the cross that we are saved amounts to nothing less than saying that Jesus was a hypocrite about his preaching.[14]

Post sees the cross as *a* way rather than *the* way of telling the Christian story of salvation. He does this because he believes that this move is required in order to establish personal communion rather than self-sacrifice as the ideal for Christian love. I do not believe that it is necessary, however, to deny the centrality of the cross in the redemptive action of God in order to maintain the position of mutuality in a Christian love ethic.

I want to propose a different approach. I suggest that we should acknowledge the place of a self-sacrificial love that is imitative of Christ's action on the cross, but that we should see this as the exception rather than the rule. There are times when a person is confronted by an environment calling for a very high level of self-giving. This is especially so in extreme situations such as a war, a context of violent oppression and/or profound deprivation, or having a loved one suffering from a chronic illness or an acute disability. In these contexts, some are able to rise to great heights of self-sacrifice. The cost might even extend to the ultimate level in some situations. In the giving of her life for the sake of others, a person reflects the self-sacrifice of Christ. But such a saintly act, while it profoundly expresses the nature of love and is deeply inspirational, does not constitute the norm for Christians. It is possible to acknowledge that some have a particular "talent" for self-sacrifice without taking the further step of establishing it as the norm. For example, I love tennis and I am deeply inspired by Roger Federer's level of ability and total dedication, but I do not see that as an ideal for me. Federer is a tennis genius and I cannot hope to get near him. There are certain individuals who have a "genius" for self-sacrificial love and I cannot hope to get near to them either. Jesus' sacrifice on the cross is a prime example of this genius for self-giving. I can state the fact that I am profoundly inspired by the level of love Christ showed on Calvary, and I can also posit the cross as absolutely central in the plan of salvation, without at the same time being compelled to uphold self-sacrifice as the ideal for Christian love.

So, though I disagree with Post on the status of the cross in God's economy of salvation, I nevertheless think that he is right in contending that it is not self-sacrifice that God has established as a norm in loving relations with others, but rather mutuality and reciprocity. We are to give and we are to receive in our communion with others and with God. To talk in terms of reciprocity does not imply selfishness, however. The disciple of Christ is required to give to others. There will be times when a giving of self is the last thing she wants to do. But to fall into a pattern of giving only when it suits her is to destroy any chance of establishing communion. Communion involves reciprocity: both the giving and the receiving need to be consistent.

SELF-SACRIFICE AND OPPRESSION

It could be argued that I have not taken us very far by following Post's lead on communion. Some might respond by saying that behind the concept of reciprocity is simply a reluctance to accept a high standard for Christian love. I do in fact believe that asking disciples to reach too high is unhelpful. Those who do not have the requisite genius for self-giving—the majority of us—will be set up for failure and will consequently suffer from an intolerable burden of guilt. It is far better to establish the normative shape of our experience of love as giving and receiving in fellowship. Indeed, as we have seen, there is strong biblical evidence suggesting that God's ideal in interaction with humans is the loving response that leads to communion.

Quite apart from the problem of setting people up for failure through imposing an unrealistic moral standard, there is arguably an even more serious concern associated with making self-sacrifice normative. Christian feminists and others with a concern for justice make the important point that those who are being oppressed are served very poorly by the notion of self-sacrificial love. If others, namely, the oppressors, were to have a change of heart and began to sacrifice some or all of their privileges, the suffering ones would obviously be well served. This, it hardly needs to be said, is an exceedingly remote possibility. The pattern that we have seen so often is one in which the oppressors give in to greed and selfishness and abuse the power associated with their position. Those in the underclass are made to sacrifice themselves for the sake of the privileged. For example, prior to the impact of feminism, generations of women passed over opportunities for education and involvement in the workforce, believing that they had no right to these things. They saw it as their calling to give of themselves so that others—namely, the men in the family—could pursue their professional calling. On the model of mutuality, women are still called to give, but they are also entitled to receive. Increasingly, we are seeing men prepared to make adjustments to their plans in order to help a partner pursue her goals. The men should not be asked to sacrifice their plans, but neither should they feel entitled to stick rigidly to what might be the ideal situation for them.

For all the reasons that I have mentioned, I believe Post is right to posit communion as the ideal for Christian love. There is an authentic self-love. There is an appropriate concern for self in which personal needs and aspirations are pursued in the context of a loving commitment to the needs and aspirations of those with whom one shares life.

SUMMARY

What I have been trying to do throughout in this chapter is to assign a proper place to self-love. In the Christian life, the ideal is communion. That is, one should feel free to pursue one's own legitimate needs and desires, but always in the context of a loving consideration of the valid concerns of others. Because for some of us all of the time, and for all of us some of the time, selfishness is a problem, we need what Outka calls "a practical swerve" in the direction of the other person and her needs. If we build in a swerve toward the other, the chances of achieving the right balance between regard for self and regard for others will be greatly improved. The ideal for the Christian is indeed communion: giving and receiving in a relationship of love. Outka's practical strategy will help to keep us out of the trap of talking about reciprocity while falling down into selfishness.

Chapter 10

The Virtues of Responsibility

Agape, we have just acknowledged, is a virtue right at the heart of the Christian life. Love, along with faith and hope, are what Thomas Aquinas calls the theological virtues. Virtue theory is one of the three basic approaches to constructing a theory of the moral life. The other two are referred to as the teleological and the deontological approaches. A teleological theory of ethics holds that an action, or the rule guiding the action, is morally right if it is likely to produce the greatest possible balance of good over evil. The teleological approach is characterized, then, by a primary concern with consequences. The term "deontology" is formed from the Greek words *deon* (duty) and *logos* (science and reason), suggesting that a moral act is performed not so much because it is likely to promote human welfare, but rather because it constitutes the fulfillment of a promise or demonstrates loyalty to a moral imperative. Although both these approaches have much to offer, I want to make use of the third approach, aretaic or virtue ethics. This approach has been around for a very long time, and has recently experienced a revival. Influential moral philosophers such as Alasdair MacIntyre, Philippa Foot, and Stuart Hampshire, and theological ethicists such as Stanley Hauerwas and Jean Porter, have turned their attention to the category of character to inform their work. In doing so, they find themselves necessarily going back to the thought of Aristotle and Aquinas. This will be our starting point also. For these thinkers, a virtue is, in essence, a habit that represents a readiness to do the good. Aquinas goes a step further than Aristotle and says that the ultimate aim of the good life is friendship with God.

The purpose in looking at some of the reflections of Aristotle and Aquinas is to help us describe exactly what we mean when we refer to

Moving Toward Spiritual Maturity
© 2007 by The Haworth Press, Inc. All rights reserved.
doi:10.1300/5886_10

virtue. It is not our purpose to attempt to discuss all the intricacies in their thought. Rather, we simply want to follow the rough outlines, to pick up the key ideas. Given that a virtue in a theological perspective is a moral habit representing conformity to God's way of love and goodness, what are the central virtues a Christian needs? Or, following the theme of this section, what are the moral excellences required for a faithful response to the material, emotional, and spiritual needs in the individuals and communities we encounter? Although there are good reasons for including virtues such as respect, fidelity, and justice, I've chosen to give attention to these three: *integrity, courage,* and *compassion.* The aim is not to be exhaustive, but in looking at these key virtues a number of central issues associated with the moral life will be raised. One such issue will be the fact that developing a virtue requires a strong will and a lasting commitment; it does not come easily or quickly. That choices in the moral life are often complex and ambiguous is a second reality that will be highlighted in our discussion. In order to lay the foundations for our explorations, we will turn to the classical statements on virtue.

ARISTOTLE ON VIRTUE

Aristotle viewed human beings, along with all other creatures, as having a specific nature. Now it is in the nature of human beings and all other creatures to move toward a specific end or goal. The human, then, has by nature an orientation to a good end. This good, says Aristotle, is happiness or blessedness *(eudaimonia).* The virtues are those dispositions, or states, which enable a person to attain happiness; the lack of which will frustrate her movement toward that goal. This blessed state that is the goal of life is indissolubly linked to the good. In moving a person toward blessedness, the virtues are efficacious because they make a person good and make him "do his own work well."[1]

Aristotle wants also to include a "pleasure principle." Contrary to the deontological approach, according to which it doesn't matter what a person is feeling as long as she fulfills her duty, the truly virtuous person in Aristotle's view both acts rightly and feels rightly. So, for example, a temperate person abstains from bodily pleasures and takes delight in that fact; a courageous person stands firm when under attack and takes pleasure in this, or at least is not distressed by the experience (*NE* 1104b4-10). Thus, rejoicing in right actions, enjoying doing the good, is essential if a person is to be considered truly virtuous.

Alongside feeling rightly, Aristotle wants to place choosing aright. Choice plays a major role in his theory of virtue. It is referred to in terms of "deliberative desire" (*NE* 1113a10-13). Aristotle here is linking reason and desire; the two must work together. Reason alone cannot move a person to act; a person turns her mind in a certain direction because she wants to. On the other hand, desire alone is insufficient to determine conduct; it must be formed by reason.

The capacity for making a good choice is possible because a person has attained the virtue of practical wisdom *(phronesis)*. A person of practical wisdom possesses both true reasoning and right desire (*NE* 1139a23-25). Reason and desire are harnessed in deliberating well in order to establish those passions and actions that conduce to the good life. In relation to passions and actions, notes Aristotle, there are three possibilities: the excess, the defect, and the intermediate or *mean* (*NE* 1106b16-28). It is possible to feel fear and confidence, anger and pity, and in general pleasure and pain, too strongly or too weakly. Moral excellence, however, involves feeling the passions "at the right times, with reference to the right objects, towards the right people, with the right aim, and in the right way" (*NE* 1106b21-22). This is the intermediate. The situation is similar in relation to action. Judgment is required in matters pertaining to moral excellence in order to establish the mean. Thus the person possessing moral excellence and the capacity for right deliberation will establish courage as the mean between fear and rashness, liberality as the mean between prodigality and meanness, proper pride as sitting midway between empty vanity and undue humility, and so on.

The person of virtue uses reason to order and tame the passions and appetites. Reason can never be the slave of passion. The moral life is fundamentally about excellent deliberation ordering the passions and so moving the moral agent toward attainment of the good. Indeed, moral excellence and practical wisdom are indissolubly linked. Moral excellence establishes the right end for the human, and practical wisdom indicates the means for achieving that end (*NE* 1145a4-6). Choice will not be right without both practical wisdom and moral excellence. It is not possible, therefore, for a person who is morally deficient to exercise practical wisdom.

The choice of what appears to be a virtuous act does not in itself guarantee that this act is in fact virtuous. A soldier may, for example, stand firm in the face of an enemy onslaught not because he is courageous, but rather because he is so overwhelmed with fear and terror that he cannot move. It is only a choice made in the context of a virtuous character that establishes an act as morally excellent. Actions may be called just and temperate when they are done as just and temperate persons do them.

Choice and practical wisdom are clearly key concepts in Aristotle's theory of moral virtue. So, finally, is the idea of *training*. Through the use of practical wisdom the moral agent is able to establish those passions and actions that over time are formative of character. It is in acting virtuously that a person eventually comes to possess this or that virtue. Just as a person becomes a lyre player by playing the lyre, one becomes just by doing just acts, brave by doing courageous acts, and so on (*NE* 1103a31-1103b1).

So what then is a virtue for Aristotle? It is "a state concerned with choice, lying in a mean relative to us, this being determined by reason in the way in which the man of practical wisdom would determine it" (*NE* 1106b36-1107a1). In looking at Aquinas' theory, we will see most of these themes emerging, but they will be reshaped through a theological orientation.

AQUINAS ON VIRTUE

Aquinas follows Aristotle in positing that the human, by nature, is oriented to a goal or end. However, he does something that his teacher was unable to do, namely, describe the role of the will in moving a person toward that goal. Furthermore, while he agrees that happiness is the proximate end for the human person, he insists that her ultimate end is supernatural. The person who has the theological as well as the natural virtues is moving toward the joy of friendship with God. That is, the virtues of faith, hope, and love need to be added to the natural excellences in order for a person to reach the end for which she or he was created.

For Aquinas, there is one overarching, ultimate end to which the actions determined by will and reason is oriented. In his *Commentary on Nichomachean Ethics,* Aquinas argues that where there are several goods identified, it is necessary to transcend the plurality in order to establish a superordinate end.[2] There is a unity in human nature and it follows that the human person's ultimate end must be one. It is possible, some would say by way of objection, to construe the tendency to orient all one's actions to the one superordinate goal, even if it is a noble one, as distorted and unbalanced. Is it not preferable to structure one's life around a series of interconnected goals? Despite what appears on the surface, Aquinas in fact intends something like this.[3] The one end incorporates a number of different goods, pursued and enjoyed in a harmonious fashion. Thus we can think of a superordinate goal and a number of subordinate goals. With this is mind, Aquinas can say that the human, if not directly seeking the perfect good, his ultimate end, is seeking a good "as tending to that, for a start is made in order to come to a finish."[4]

Aquinas believes that every person naturally acts in such a way as to pursue what she perceives as the good.[5] Clearly, it is possible for a person to be mistaken about what is good for her. But no one—no one who is of sound mind, that is—intentionally acts against the good. This is because we are all oriented by nature to the goal of happiness. Once a person becomes aware that a certain action or practice is not in fact good for her, she will make the requisite change in her behavior.

So the human person is essentially oriented to the good; she chooses acts that her reason tells her will move her toward the goal of happiness. Virtue, according to Aquinas (and following Aristotle), is that which makes the agent good and her acts also good (*ST* I-II.56.3). It is virtue, then, that disposes a person to act well, in accordance with her essential orientation to the end for which she was created. The question is, though, how does a person acquire virtue? Aquinas asks whether a virtuous disposition can be acquired through a single act (*ST* I-II.51.3). Clearly this is not possible. In order for virtue to become established in a person, reason must achieve mastery over desire. Now there are many, many situations involving a vast number of factors in which the passions come into play. It is not possible to establish right and good judgments in all these complex and diverse situations "in an instant," so to speak. The virtuous disposition develops over time; it is a *habit*. It is a complicated business managing one's desires in order to establish virtue. A young business executive, for example, finds that there are a number of ways in which she can advance herself at the expense of others. She resists the temptation for a whole year and feels that she can now say that she has the virtue of justice. The problem is, though, that the temptation can surface in so many different forms. It is only through breadth of experience and through consistently choosing the right and good path that the virtue takes root.

As Stanley Hauerwas points out, though, Aquinas' notion of a habit is quite different from our modern idea.[6] We tend to think of a habit in terms of a routine action. One has the habit, for example, of each day buying a newspaper on the way home from work, reading it, and then walking the dog. For Aquinas, in contrast, a habit is a disposition to act well (or ill). So when he speaks of a virtue as a habit, he refers to a well-established disposition to act for the good. According to Hauerwas, habits are a "readiness for action" (p. 70). I find myself in a situation where I am required to act justly, or courageously, and, having the virtue of justice or courage formed in me, I am ready to respond.

In our discussion on Aristotle's account of the virtues, we saw that choice and practical reason are key functions. What we did not see mentioned is the role of the *will*. This omission constitutes a weakness in Aristotle's theory. Aquinas, for his part, assigns the will a very important place in his moral psychology in general and in his theory of virtue, in particular. He says that the intellect is moved by the will, as all human faculties are (*ST* I-II.56.3). A person turns her mind in a certain direction because that is what she wants to do. The intellect, in this sense, is subordinate to the will. Thus, will is the subject of "virtue in its unqualified sense" (*ST* I-II.56.3). The moral virtues are oriented to the will, and the intellectual virtues to the rational powers. This has significant practical import. There is a big difference between saying, "I would like to act justly," on the one hand, and, "I *will* do what justice demands of me," on the other. It is only when the will is engaged that a person is able to enact the good.

Let me try to pull together a few of the main threads in these classic discussions on virtue. The aim of the life of virtue is to conform oneself to the good. This is not something that comes easily, but rather something that requires discipline and effort. For Aristotle, it is primarily a matter of disciplining oneself to follow the path dictated by both reason and desire. Aquinas finds it important to emphasize the role of the will. The desire to act viciously may be strong, but through engaging the will I can choose to act virtuously. If I am consistent in acting for the good, it is habit-forming. That is, even though it is quite hard initially to act virtuously, the more I do so, the easier it gets. The reason that I am prepared to struggle to form the habit is that I am aiming at an extremely worthwhile goal. While both Aristotle and Aquinas agree that that goal is happiness, the latter adds that the ultimate goal is friendship with God.

THE VIRTUOUS CHRISTIAN

I want now to turn our attention to three vitally important moral habits for those of us who are on the Christian way, namely integrity, courage, and compassion. In the course of our reflections, we will pick up on some of the key ideas developed by the classic virtue ethicists. These three are not, of course, the only virtues required. Fidelity, justice, and respect, to name just a few others, are also very necessary. In choosing the three that I have, the aim is not to be exhaustive, but rather to explore some of the issues and concerns associated with growing into virtue. One such issue relates to the fact that virtues are habits. Since this is the case, unless one works at them consistently they very quickly and easily fall away. Another issue is complexity and ambiguity. It is often not clear which of the courses open to us represents, for example, the way of integrity. I hope to highlight these and other issues in the ensuing discussion.

Integrity

The pastoral theologian Alastair Campbell has a helpful way of talking about integrity. He writes:

> To possess integrity is to be incapable of compromising that which we believe to be true. . . . To possess integrity is to have a kind of inner strength which prevents us from bending to the influence of what is thought expedient, or fashionable or calcu-

lated to win praise; it is to be consistent and utterly trustworthy because of a constancy of purpose.[7]

Here Campbell sets fidelity to convictions and personal consistency against desire for popularity and capitulation to expediency. As Christians, we find ourselves constantly in situations in which we have to choose truthfulness and consistency over popularity. In the school and the university, in the church, and in the working world we are called on to own our personal truths. There may be times when we consider it strategic to remain silent, or to tone down our message. While this is sometimes appropriate, the virtue theorists remind us that herein lies a danger. What started as a strategic approach can soon develop into a vicious habit. Whereas once we were able to consistently live in and through our personal truth, slowly but surely we find this virtue being weakened. Over time, we find ourselves valuing popularity too highly. We find it more and more difficult to speak our truth plainly. Strategy has turned into vice.

A number of psychologists refer to the true or authentic self and the false or conforming self. They contend that values are the primary factor in establishing a coherent sense of selfhood.[8] The suggestion is that when a person acts in accordance with her value structure she feels in touch with her core self. That is to say, living true to her deepest values leads to a sense of authenticity. A person whose words and actions are congruent with her value structure feels as though she is living out of her true self. Such authentic living is difficult to enact, of course.

Because there are large benefits that accrue from conforming to the wishes and desires of others, especially popularity and praise, many of us find that over time we lose touch to an extent with our real selves. We have become so used to responding to the question, "What do they want me to say?" that we too often fail to ask, "What do I believe?" Another way of talking about the virtue of integrity is to say that it belongs to those who live out of their real selves. What matters most to persons of integrity are these two things. First, they value getting in touch with their own deepest ideas, values, and convictions. And second, they put a high priority on putting those ideas and values before others. It is possible to fail at either point. Some of us, for instance, have become so habituated to an inner dialogue dominated by external demands that we no longer have access to our deepest beliefs. In a moment of scary self-discovery, we are hit with the aware-ness of a loss of self-contact. We realize that we have no immediate contact with a personal center.

It may be, on the other hand, that a person is able to access his per-sonal beliefs quite readily, but is too afraid to speak out. In his book *Who is Worthy?* Father Ted Kennedy opens his deeply challenging re-flections on the Church's relationship to gay people and to the Aus-tralian indigenous community with this comment:

> Some time ago I suffered a stroke which triggered in me a deci-sion to live the rest of my life as if I were already dead. I am now more inclined to state things as they are, or as I see them, with-out fear or compromise.[9]

The problem for many of us is that we can't achieve this illusion. We are very aware of being alive, and we are even more aware of the liv-ing hell others may wish to create for us!

The virtue ethicists do not, of course, have any easy answers to offer here. Developing the virtue of integrity is demanding work. The guidance that is offered is that the will needs to be engaged if we are to avoid a fall away from consistency and trustworthiness. As noted earlier, there is a significant difference between desire and will. Will is a much stronger mental and spiritual capacity. Many of us share Ted Kennedy's desire to "state things as they are," whatever that may mean for us personally, but we lack the will that he has shown. Desire guides our actions, but not nearly as decisively as the will. Once the will has been fully engaged, the course has been set. A person grow-ing in integrity needs a strong will lest she be pulled away by fear or compromise.

Courage

All of this highlights the fact that there is a very close relationship between integrity and courage. It takes courage to consistently express our personal truths. Indeed, Christians need a certain kind of tough-ness. It is a toughness out of which we are able to speak the hard word. The strength that I am referring to here needs to be understood in the context of Christ's strength. When he spoke out in the name of truth, it was never with the aim of self-promotion or any other form of self-aggrandizement. There is a way of being tough that is self-grounded, but what I am describing is a strength used for the sake of the common good.

There is another side to this toughness. It is important to be able to form a reasonably hard exterior. There is a good reason that we so often fail to hold to our personal truth, namely, others make us pay a high price. If we are to develop a strong capacity to speak the truth when others don't want to hear it, we need to develop a firm exterior that is able to stop the hurtful comments from penetrating too deeply. The firmness I have in mind sits midway between a soft, porous exterior and a hard-baked, impenetrable one. The hard-baked personality is familiar to us. Nothing seems to be able to find its way through his or her rock-like exterior. But we also know that he or she has little or no compassion—a virtue that is at the heart of the Christian life, and one that we will be discussing shortly. Persons with a soft outer layer, on the other hand, may quite readily reach out to others with tender kindness, but they suffer in truth-telling through allowing too many harsh words to get into their system. In the end, the cost associated with courageous words will likely be judged to be too high. The challenges and taunts of their opponents are allowed to "move in." Like unwelcome guests, they take up residence and make life for the reluctant host almost unbearable. In the middle of the night, they make their presence felt and sleep becomes impossible. They are there in the morning, at noontime, and right through the day. What is required is a firm exterior capable of stopping the "intruders" from penetrating too deeply, but not so hard-baked that one loses sensitivity to others.

We have been reflecting on the courage to speak one's personal truth. There is a most interesting case of this in Galatians 2 involving the Apostle Peter. It centers on the issue of table fellowship with Gentiles. In order to understand the nature of Peter's struggle, we need to turn our attention to Acts 10. Here we read the story of the revolution in Peter's thinking through which God opened him to fellowship with Gentile Christians. God had directed the Roman centurion and God-fearer, Cornelius, to send for Peter at Jaffa. While the messengers were on the way, Peter had a vision. In his vision, he was confronted by what looked like a big sheet filled with all kinds of creatures. Peter was commanded by the Lord to kill and eat that which was before him. When he objected on the grounds of his concern for ritual purity, a voice declared to him, "What God has made clean, you have no right to call profane" (v. 15). Through this dramatic experience, Peter learned the revolutionary lesson that "God does not have favorites" and "anybody of any nationality who fears God and does what is right is acceptable to him" (v. 35). He did indeed make the trip to visit with Cornelius and his household.

Not surprisingly, there were Jewish Christians in Jerusalem who were less than happy with Peter's behavior. It is difficult for us to grasp how scandalous his actions must have seemed to the brethren. Here was one of their leaders flaunting their cherished ancestral traditions. They chastised him thus: "So you have been visiting the uncircumcised and eating with them, have you?" (Acts 11:3-4). Peter responded courageously. He did not recant; but, instead, simply told them the incredible story of his "conversion."

With this background before us, it is puzzling to read Paul's account in Galatians 2:11-14 of his clash with Peter in Antioch over this very same issue. It seems that Peter did a u-turn when he was put under pressure.

> When Cephas came to Antioch, however, I opposed him to his face, since he was manifestly in the wrong. His custom had been to eat with pagans, but after certain friends of James arrived he stopped doing this and kept away from them altogether for fear of the group that insisted on circumcision. The other Jews joined him in this pretence, and even Barnabas felt himself obliged to copy his behavior.

> When I saw they were not respecting the true meaning of the Good News, I said to Cephas in front of everyone, "In spite of being a Jew, you live like the pagans and not like the Jews, so you have no right to make the pagans copy Jewish ways."

Given this account, it might seem that Paul had every right to attack Peter. The latter capitulated because he was afraid of the circumcision party. But we do only have one version of the incident. How would Peter have defended himself? "He would have claimed," suggests F. F. Bruce, "that he acted out of consideration for the weaker brethren—the weaker brethren on this occasion being those back home in Jerusalem."[10] This points to the fact, I think, that it is not always clear what it means to act with integrity. It may indeed have been that Peter was not so much acting out of fear, but rather out of a concern for those Jewish Christians who were vulnerable, who were not yet secure enough in their faith to cope with such a momentous challenge.

Here a different aspect of courage also comes into view. When faced with a complex and ambiguous situation, it takes real courage to act. There is always the fear that one will take the wrong option. To reverse the course sometimes involves a loss of face. Others will condemn you with complaints of weakness and capitulation to pressure. When Peter was forced to rethink his position after hearing the concerns of the "friends of James," he realized, we may presume, that while he felt free in himself to fellowship with Gentiles, his high profile in the Jesus movement meant that he must accord a strong weightage to the possibility that his actions might work against the consolidation of the faith of the weaker brethren. With this latter concern very much in mind, he pulled back from his new liberated practice.

Was Peter being courageous in making this change? Or was Paul right after all to assert that he simply caved in under pressure? As Christians, we live with similar tensions as does Peter. It is often not clear which course of action is the one that is marked by integrity. To act at all when the situation is murky and confused, shows a certain level of courage. It is also true that to effect a reversal when it seems necessary requires inner strength. We don't like to have to admit that perhaps we had not thought the issue through fully enough. Moreover, we find it difficult to cope with the criticism of those favoring the first approach.

Compassion

The final virtue for the Christian life that I want to reflect on is compassion. If we need a certain toughness in order to remain faithful to our vocation, we also need a type of softness. It is important, as I mentioned earlier, to be able to keep out the harsh words of others. But we also need a kind of "porousness," if you will, that allows us to feel another's pain and distress.[11]

We have seen that Aquinas stresses the importance of the will in developing virtue. But can we *will* ourselves to feel compassion?

Clearly we cannot. What we *can* do is to open ourselves to let the suffering of the other in. Since we are bombarded daily with so much human need and distress, both in personal encounters and through the media, there is a danger that we will seal ourselves off. What is required, in fact, is a partial sealing off. We cannot respond compassionately to every stimulus that comes our way. Rather, we have to respond selectively. There will be some looks, certain words, particular pleas that we know we have to open ourselves to. We feel ourselves under a pull—the tug of the Holy Spirit—to offer ourselves.

At this point the will becomes vitally important. Of course we *want* to help. We cannot deny that we have felt God nudging us. But it takes mental, emotional, and physical energy to make our response. To get us moving, to do that which must be done, requires a strong will. In the course of time, if we continually put the will to work, a pattern of compassionate response develops. We find that we have within us a readiness to act compassionately. This is the virtue of compassion taking root.

It is interesting to observe this readiness to act, this habit of compassion, in that icon of loving service, the Good Samaritan. Clearly this habit was not strongly ingrained in either the priest or the Levite. It is not stated why they passed by on the other side. It may have been that they were afraid of becoming contaminated through contact with what they took to be a dead body. Or perhaps they were hesitant about an encounter with one of the lowly "people of the land." In any case, the readiness to help a person in need that may have been part of their moral character was not strong enough to override other concerns. The Samaritan himself, of course, had a major concern, namely that the injured man was a member of the hated Jewish race. Almost miraculously, one might say, he was able to break through that barrier; such was the strength of his compassion and desire to help.

SUMMARY

What I have been attempting to do is to use the virtue ethics approach to describe the moral character of the Christian. Looking to Aristotle and Aquinas, we saw that a virtue is a habit that moves a person toward the goal of happiness. To establish a particular virtue does not come easily or quickly. One must train oneself in the way of virtue. One becomes just, for example, by engaging in just acts. Over time, the habit of justice is formed in a person so that she has a readiness to act justly when the occasion calls for it.

While I could have picked other virtues to concentrate on, I chose integrity, courage, and compassion. Through the discussion, I wanted to show that it is indeed a hard struggle to develop the virtuous self. To live consistently in and through a personal truth is a very demanding vocation. The lures of expediency and popularity are very strong. The same is true of the challenge of responding compassionately. There is an ever-present temptation to seal oneself off from the suffering of others.

I also wanted to indicate some of the complexity associated with the virtuous life. It is not always clear what constitutes the good and right action. It is difficult enough to find the will to act once a course has been established. But what makes the moral life especially demanding is the fact that it sometimes requires significant courage even to make a decision about a course of action.

Notes

Introduction

1. For an excellent treatment of an integrated approach to helping persons with psychospiritual formation, see L. Sperry, *Transforming Self and Community: Revisioning Pastoral Counseling and Spiritual Direction* (Collegeville, MN: Liturgical Press, 2002).

Chapter 1

1. See A. Maslow, *The Farther Reaches of Human Nature* (Harmondsworth: Penguin Books, 1973), p. 29.

2. Most talk in terms of an immanent rather than a transcendent spirituality. That is, the focus of the spiritual side of life for them is on the inner self and on interpersonal life, not on a relationship with a transcendent Being.

3. See J. Fowler, *Becoming Adult, Becoming Christian* (Melbourne: Dove Communications, 1984), p. 101.

4. Maslow, *Farther Reaches,* p. 33.

5. Ibid., p. 51.

6. See ibid., p. 48.

7. Ibid., p. 49.

8. R. May, *Man's Search for Himself* (London: Souvenir Press, 1975), p. 160.

9. Ibid., p. 161.

10. See D. Rowe, *Wanting Everything: The Art of Happiness* (London: Fontana, 1991), p. 341.

11. Ibid., p. 340.

12. May, *Man's Search,* p. 165.

13. Maslow, *Farther Reaches,* p. 48.

14. May, *Man's Search,* p. 224.

15. Ibid., p. 224.

16. Ibid., p. 157.

17. Ibid., pp. 251-252.

18. See Rowe, *Wanting Everything,* p. 347.

19. Ibid., p. 347.

20. See ibid., p. 361.

Moving Toward Spiritual Maturity
© 2007 by The Haworth Press, Inc. All rights reserved.
doi:10.1300/5886_11

21. See R. May, *Love and Will* (New York: W.W. Norton, 1969), pp. 317-319.

22. See Maslow, *Farther Reaches,* p. 138ff.

23. Fowler, *Becoming Adult, Becoming Christian,* p. 101.

24. G. Badcock, *The Way of Life: A Theology of Christian Vocation* (Grand Rapids: Eerdmans, 1998), pp. 72-73.

25. R. C. Roberts, "The Troubled Self—Me, Myself, & I: How Far Should We Go in Our Search for Self-Fulfillment?" *Christianity Today* 37, no. 7 (June 21, 1993), p. 37.

26. See Badcock, *Way of Life,* p. 113ff.

27. Ibid., p. 116.

28. Ibid., p. 112.

Chapter 2

1. This is a point that the leading pastoral theologian Don Browning has made often. See, for example, his *The Moral Context of Care* (Philadelphia: Westminster Press, 1976), and *Religious Ethics and Pastoral Care* (Minneapolis: Fortress Press, 1983).

2. See J. Rowan, *Subpersonalities: The People Inside Us* (London: Routledge, 1990), p. 46ff.

3. Ibid., p. 8.

4. Ibid., p. 198.

5. Ibid., p. 48.

6. See ibid., p. 196.

7. See J. M. M. Mair, "The Community of Self," in D. Bannister, ed., *New Perspectives in Personal Construct Theory* (London: Academic Press, 1977), pp. 125-149.

8. See H. Markus and P. Nurius, "Possible Selves," *American Psychologist* 41, no. 9 (September 1986), pp. 954-969.

9. Ibid., p. 954.

10. Here we should note that Berne points out that while Freud's three psychic agencies—id, ego, and superego—are theoretical constructs, his Parent, Adult, and Child ego states are real. That is, we do actually experience these states in everyday life. Further, the notion of the unconscious is completely dropped by Berne. This means that the Child is not an instinctual phenomenon. Finally, the cultural dimension that is strongly associated with the superego is not emphasized by Berne in relation to the Parent.

11. See T. Harris, *I'm Okay—You're Okay* (London: Jonathan Cape, 1973), p. 16.

12. See E. Berne, *Beyond Games and Scripts* (New York: Grove Press, 1976), p. 159.

13. See M. Hoskins and J. Leseho, "Changing Metaphors of the Self: Implications for Counseling," *Journal of Counseling and Development* 74, no. 3 (January-February 1996), pp. 243-252.

14. H. Kohut, *The Restoration of the Self* (New York: International Universities Press, 1977), p. 18.

15. See H. Kohut, "Remarks About the Formation of the Self: Letter to a Student Regarding Some Principles of Psychoanalytic Research," in P. Orstein, ed., *The*

Search for the Self, vol. 2 (New York: International Universities Press, 1978), pp. 737-770, p. 757.

16. See Kohut, *Restoration of the Self,* p. 171.

17. See C. G. Jung, *Aion,* 2nd ed., 5th printing (Princeton, NJ: Princeton University Press, 1978), p. 8.

18. Ibid., p. 14.

19. Ibid., p. 8.

20. Ibid.

21. Ibid., p. 9.

22. See J. Bradshaw, *Healing the Shame That Binds You* (Deerfield Beach: Health Communications, 1988), p. 148ff.

23. Ibid., p. 148.

24. Ibid., p. 149.

25. See ibid., p. 150ff.

26. Ibid., pp. 150-151.

27. Jung, *Aion,* p. 8.

28. See H. Stone and S. Winkelman, *Embracing Our Selves* (Marina del Rey, CA: Devorss and Co., 1985).

29. Bradshaw, *Healing the Shame,* p. 145.

30. Jung, *Aion,* p. 8.

Chapter 3

1. J. Andrew Overman, *Church and Community in Crisis: The Gospel According to Matthew* (Valley Forge, PA: Trinity Press International, 1996), p. 83.

2. Ibid., p. 83.

3. C. G. Jung, *Two Essays in Analytical Psychology,* 2nd ed. (Princeton, NJ: Princeton University Press, 1972), p. 173.

4. Ibid., p. 173.

5. Along with Jung's own work, I found Hall and Nordby's primer most useful in preparing this summary of Jungian psychology. See C. S. Hall and V. J. Nordby, *A Primer of Jungian Psychology* (New York: Mentor, 1973).

6. C. G. Jung, *Aion,* 2nd ed., 5th printing (Princeton, NJ: Princeton University Press, 1978), pp. 1-2.

7. C. G. Jung, *Man and His Symbols* (London: Picador, 1978), p. 11. First published in 1964.

8. Cf. Hall and Nordby, *A Primer,* p. 37.

9. C. G. Jung, *Psychological Reflections* (London: Routledge and Kegan Paul, 1971), p. 39.

10. Cf. Hall and Nordby, *A Primer,* p. 41.

11. Jung, *Man and His Symbols,* p. 58.

12. Jung, *Aion,* p. 7.

13. See ibid., Ch. 5.

14. Ibid., p. 37.

15. See ibid., p. 63.

16. Ibid., p. 63.

17. Ibid., p. 68.

18. Ibid.

19. Ibid., pp. 68-69.

20. Ibid., p. 69.

21. See E. Käsemann, *Commentary on Romans* (Grand Rapids: Eerdmans, 1980), p. 204.

22. See L. Morris, *The Epistle to the Romans* (Grand Rapids: Eerdmans, 1988), p. 295.

23. See ibid., p. 293.

24. Ibid., p. 291.

25. S. Mayer, "High-Risk Perfectionism," *Human Development* 20, no. 1 (Spring 1999), pp. 5-8, p. 8.

26. Jung, *Aion,* p. 266.

27. M.-L. von Franz, "The Process of Individuation," in Jung, *Man and His Symbols,* p. 182.

28. K. Bingaman also makes this point. See his "Christianity and the Shadow Side of Human Experience," *Pastoral Psychology* 49, no. 3 (January 2001), pp. 167-180, p. 172.

29. Jung, *Psychological Reflections,* p. 240.

30. Käsemann, *Commentary,* p. 210.

Chapter 4

1. See R. Karen, "Shame," *Atlantic Monthly* (February 1992), pp. 40-70.

2. R. Hutch, "Confessing Dying Within," *Journal of Pastoral Care* 48, no. 4 (Winter 1994), pp. 341-352, p. 351. Used with permission.

3. H. B. Lewis, *Shame and Guilt in Neurosis* (New York: International Universities Press, 1971), p. 36.

4. S. Pattison, *Shame: Theory, Therapy, Theology* (New York: Cambridge University Press, 2000), p. 62.

5. The term "situational shame" comes from R. Karen. See his "Shame."

6. See E. Erikson, *Identity: Youth and Crisis* (New York: W.W. Norton, 1968).

7. Ibid., p. 127.

8. Cf. W. Au and N. Cannon, "The Plague of Perfectionism," *Human Development* 13, no. 3 (Fall 1992), pp. 5-12, p. 5.

9. See ibid., p. 119.

10. J. Beck, *Cognitive Therapy: Basics and Beyond* (New York: The Guilford Press, 1995), p. 16.

11. See ibid., p. 109.

12. See S. Jones, "Rational-Emotive Therapy in Christian Perspective," *Journal of Psychology and Theology* 17 (Summer 1989), pp. 110-120.

13. A. Jones, *Exploring Spiritual Direction* (Cambridge, MA: Cowley Publications, 1982, 1999), p. 147.

14. David Burns has shown how this can be done. See his *Feeling Good: The New Mood Therapy* (New York: Morrow, 1980).

15. On uselessness in the Christian life, see Jones, *Exploring Spiritual Direction,* p. 136.

16. S. Mayer, "High-Risk Perfectionism," *Human Development* 20, no. 1 (Spring 1999), pp. 5-8, p. 6.

Chapter 5

1. T. Moore, "Spiritualities of Depth," *Tikkun* 13, no. 6 (November/December 1998), pp. 40-41, p. 41.

2. See E. Dreyer, *Earth Crammed with Heaven* (New York: Paulist Press, 1994), pp. 75-76.

3. T. Merton, *Conjectures of a Guilty Bystander* (Garden City, NY: Double Day, Image Books, 1968), p. 157.

4. Moore, "Spiritualities of Depth," p. 41.

5. E. Peterson, *Working the Angles* (Grand Rapids: Eerdmans, 1987), p. 81.

6. J. Batz, "It's Hard to Understand the Nature of Nature," *National Catholic Reporter* 37, no. 8 (December 15, 2000), p. 16.

7. Chief Luther Standing Bear, My Indian Boyhood. Cited in R. Pazola, "Sacred: What Native Americans Believe," *U.S. Catholic* 59, no. 2 (February 1994), pp. 16-23, p. 16.

8. J. Nangle, "A Spirituality of Ecology," *Sojourners* 27, no. 5 (September/October 1998), p. 54.

9. Cf. D. Burton-Christie, "Into the Body of Another: Eros, Embodiment and Intimacy with the Natural World," *Anglican Theological Review* 81, no. 1 (Winter 1999), pp. 13-37.

10. P. Avis, *Eros and the Sacred* (London: SPCK, 1989), p. 129.

11. R. Banks, *All the Business of Life* (Sydney: Albatross Books, 1987), p. 71.

12. Ibid., p. 63.

13. For an extended discussion of the changes in the way marriage and family life has been envisioned and enacted, see B. Grant, *The Social Structure of Christian Families* (St. Louis: Chalice Press, 2000), pp. 129-154.

14. J. H. Rubio, *A Christian Theology of Marriage and Family* (New York: Paulist Press, 2003), p. 99.

15. See B. J. Miller-McLemore, *Also a Mother* (Nashville: Abingdon Press, 1994), pp. 110-130.

16. Ibid., pp. 122-123.

17. L. Howe, "The Family God Intends," *Journal of Pastoral Care* 53, no. 3 (Fall 1999), pp. 285-293, p. 292.

18. E. Dreyer, *Earth Crammed*, p. 80.

19. Cited in B. Stone, *Compassionate Ministry* (Maryknoll: Orbis Books, 1996), p. 60.

Chapter 6

1. I am indebted to Alan Jones for recording this telling insight into human existence. See his *Exploring Spiritual Direction* (Cambridge, MA: Cowley Publications, 1982, 1999), pp. 103-104.

2. W. Percy, *The Second Coming* (New York: Farrar, Straus and Giroux, 1980), p. 123.

3. Jones, *Exploring Spiritual Direction,* p. 108.

4. T. Merton, *Seeds of Contemplation* (London: Burns and Oates, 1949, 1957), p. 8.

5. Ibid., p. 11.

6. T. Merton, *Conjectures of a Guilty Bystander* (New York: Image Books, 1968, 1989), p. 224.

7. Ibid., p. 224.

8. T. Merton, *Contemplative Prayer* (New York: Image Books, 1971, 1996), p. 24.

9. T. Merton, *The New Man* (New York: Farrar, Straus and Giroux, 1961, 2000), p. 23.

10. Ibid., p. 102.

11. Merton, *Contemplative Prayer,* p. 97.

12. See ibid., p. 101.

13. See T. Merton, *New Seeds of Contemplation* (London: Burns and Oates, 1961), p. 45.

14. Merton, *New Seeds,* p. 13.

15. See ibid., p. 14.

16. Ibid.

17. Merton, *New Seeds,* p. 123.

18. See Merton, *New Man,* pp. 168-169.

19. Ibid., pp. 126-127.

20. Merton, *Conjectures,* p. 77.

21. Cf. A. Carr, *A Search for Wisdom and Spirit: Thomas Merton's Theology of Self* (Notre Dame, IN: University of Notre Dame Press, 1988), p. 26.

22. T. Merton, *Contemplation in a World of Action* (Notre Dame, IN: University of Notre Dame Press, 1998, 2003), p. 141.

23. Ibid., p. 153.

24. See ibid.

25. H. Nouwen, *Reaching Out* (Garden City, NY: Doubleday, 1975).

26. See E. Becker, *The Denial of Death* (New York: Free Press, 1973).

27. Ibid., p. 86.

28. Ibid., p. 30.

29. Ibid., p. 51.

30. See D. Hassel, *Radical Prayer* (New York: Paulist Press, 1983), Ch. 2.

31. Ibid., p. 23.

32. Ibid., p. 25.

33. Ibid., p. 30.

34. Nouwen, *Reaching Out,* p. 25.

35. See W. Callahan, *Noisy Contemplation* (Hyattsville, MD: Quixote Center, 1983).

36. Jones, *Exploring Spiritual Direction,* p. 99.

Chapter 7

1. B. Stone, *Compassionate Ministry* (Maryknoll: Orbis Books, 1996), p. 78.

2. See G. Little, *Strong Leadership* (Melbourne: Oxford University Press, 1988).

3. Ibid., p. 6.

4. I have also discussed the biblical notion of compassion in my book, *The Art of Listening* (Grand Rapids: Eerdmans, 2002). There I'm interested in what it has to say about our understanding of pastoral care and counseling.

5. See D. Bergant, "Compassion," in C. Stuhlmueller, ed., *The Collegeville Pastoral Dictionary of Biblical Theology* (Collegeville, MN: The Liturgical Press, 1996), pp. 154-157, p. 154.

6. See ibid., p. 154.

7. X. Leon-Dufour, "Mercy," in *Dictionary of Biblical Theology,* 2nd ed., updated, trans. P. Cahilland E. Stewart (London: Geoffrey Chapman, 1988), pp. 351-354, p. 351.

8. See Bergant, "Compassion," p. 156.

9. This discussion of *splánchnon* in pre-NT and NT usage is informed by H. Köster, "Splánchnon" in G. Kittel and G. Friedrich, eds., *Theological Dictionary of the New Testament,* vol. 1, ed., trans. G. Bromiley (Grand Rapids: Eerdmans, 1985), pp. 1067-1069.

10. Ibid., p. 1068.

11. Ibid.

12. See T. Collins, "The Physiology of Tears in the Old Testament: Part I," *Catholic Biblical Quarterly* 33 (1971), pp. 18-38.

13. See ibid., pp. 30-31.

14. Ibid., p. 38.

15. See H. Nouwen, *The Wounded Healer* (Garden City, NY: Doubleday, 1972), p. 91ff.

16. Ibid., p. 92.

17. Ibid., p. 95.

18. See P. Hanson, *The People Called: The Growth of Community in the Bible* (San Francisco: Harper & Row, 1986).

19. See ibid., p. 3.

20. Ibid., pp. 72-73.

21. Ibid., p. 402.

22. *Music in the Listening Place* is an unpublished manuscript. Quotes used with permission of author.

23. Ibid.

24. Ibid.

25. Ibid.

26. H. Nouwen, D. McNeill, and D. Morrison, *Compassion* (London: Darton, Longman and Todd, 1982), p. 108.

27. Ibid.

28. Ibid., p. 110.

Chapter 8

1. See R. Gula, "Conscience," in B. Hoose, ed., *Christian Ethics: An Introduction* (London: Cassell, 1998), pp. 110-122, p. 113.

2. On the confusion between the superego and the mature conscience, see R. Gula, *Reason Informed by Faith* (Mahwah, NJ: Paulist Press, 1989), p. 123ff; and Gula, "Conscience," pp. 112-113.

3. Gula, *Reason*, p. 124.

4. S. Hauerwas, *Vision and Virtue* (Notre Dame, IN: University of Notre Dame Press, 1981), p. 2.

5. See ibid., p. 30.

6. Ibid., p. 34.

7. See B. Johnstone, "Solidarity and Moral Conscience: Challenges for our Theological and Pastoral Work," *Studia Moralia* 31 (1993), pp. 65-85, p. 66. The idea of the "contrast experience" comes from E. Schillebeeckx. Johnstone suggests that such an experience may stimulate conscience and lead to action aimed at improving the situation.

8. See C. Plantinga, *Not the Way It's Supposed to Be: A Breviary of Sin* (Grand Rapids: Eerdmans,1995), Ch. 1.

9. T. Malone, "Self-Fulfillment Through Service to Others," *The Humanist* 49, no. 1 (January 1989), p. 49.

10. Cited in Malone, "Self-Fulfillment," p. 49.

Chapter 9

1. See G. Outka, *Agape: An Ethical Analysis* (New Haven: Yale University Press, 1972).

2. See A. Nygren, *Agape and Eros: Part I* (London: SPCK, 1932); and Nygren, *Agape and Eros: Part II* (London: SPCK, 1939).

3. E. Vacek, *Love, Human and Divine: The Heart of Christian Ethics* (Washington, DC: Georgetown University Press, 1994), p. 162.

4. See Outka, *Agape,* esp. pp. 9-16 and 290-291, and G. Outka, "Universal Love and Impartiality," in E. Santuri and W. Werpehowski, eds., *The Love Commandments: Essays in Christian Ethics and Moral Philosophy* (Washington: Georgetown University Press, 1992), pp. 1-103.

5. See D. Browning, *Religious Thought and the Modern Psychologies* (Philadephia: Fortress Press, 1987), pp. 150-156; and D. Browning and C. Browning, "The Church and the Family Crisis: A New Love Ethic," *The Christian Century* 108, no. 23 (August 7, 1991), pp. 746-749.

6. See Outka, "Universal Love and Impartiality."

7. See Browning and Browning, "The Church and the Family Crisis," p. 749.

8. See Outka, "Universal Love and Impartiality," p. 4ff.

9. See ibid., p. 80ff.

10. S. Post, "The Inadequacy of Selflessness," *Journal of the American Academy of Religion* 56, no. 2 (1989), pp. 213-228, p. 213.

11. S. Post, "Communion and True Self-Love," *Journal of Religious Ethics* 16 (Fall 1988), pp. 345-362, p. 345.

12. Ibid., p. 345.

13. Post, "The Inadequacy," p. 216.

14. R. Westley, *Redemptive Intimacy,* pp. 114-115; cited in Post, "The Inadequacy," p. 220.

Chapter 10

1. See Aristotle, *Nichomachean Ethics* 1106a, 21. Henceforth to be referred to in the text as *NE.*

2. T. Aquinas, *Commentary on Nichomachean Ethics* I, lect. 9, in M. Clark, ed., *An Aquinas Reader* (New York: Fordham University Press, 1988), p. 346.

3. Cf. J. Porter, *The Recovery of Virtue: The Relevance of Aquinas for Christian Ethics* (Louisville: Westminster/John Knox Press, 1990), p. 78.

4. *Summa Theologiae* I-II.1.6. Henceforth to be referred to in the text as *ST.*

5. See T. Aquinas, *On Truth* 22.1.c, in *Aquinas Reader,* p. 257.

6. See S. Hauerwas, *Character and the Christian Life* (San Antonio: Trinity University Press, 1975), pp. 69-70.

7. A. Campbell, *Rediscovering Pastoral Care,* 2nd ed. (London: Darton, Longman and Todd, 1986), p. 12.

8. See S. Hitlin, "Values As the Core of Personal Identity: Drawing Links Between Two Theories of Self," *Social Psychology Quarterly* 66, no. 2 (June 2003), pp. 118-137.

9. T. Kennedy, *Who Is Worthy?* (Sydney: Pluto Press, 2000), p. 27.

10. F. F. Bruce, *Commentary on Galatians* (Exeter: The Paternoster Press, 1982), p. 133.

11. Gabriel Marcel observes that availability to the other requires a certain kind of "incohesion." See "Phenomenological Notes on Being in a Situation," in his *Creative Fidelity* (New York: The Noonday Press, 1964), p. 88.

Bibliography

Aquinas, T., *Summa Theologiae,* trans. T. Gilby (London: Eyre & Spottiswoode, 1964, 1965).

———, *Commentary on Nichomachean Ethics I,* lect. 9, in M. Clark, ed., *An Aquinas Reader* (New York: Fordham University Press, 1988).

———, *On Truth,* in M. Clark, ed., *An Aquinas Reader* (New York: Fordham University Press, 1988).

Aristotle, *Aristotle's Nichomachean Ethics,* trans. Hippocrates G. Apostle (Grinelli, IA: The Peripatetic Press, 1984).

Au, W. and Cannon, N., "The Plague of Perfectionism," *Human Development* 13, no. 3 (Fall 1992), pp. 5-12.

Avis, P., *Eros and the Sacred* (London: SPCK, 1989).

Badcock, G., *The Way of Life: A Theology of Christian Vocation* (Grand Rapids: Eerdmans, 1998).

Banks, R., *All the Business of Life* (Sydney: Albatross Books, 1987).

Batz, J., "It's Hard to Understand the Nature of Nature," *National Catholic Reporter* 37, no. 8 (December 15, 2000), p. 16.

Beck, J., *Cognitive Therapy: Basics and Beyond* (New York: The Guilford Press, 1995).

Becker, E., *The Denial of Death* (New York: Free Press, 1973).

Bergant, D., "Compassion," in C. Stuhlmueller, ed., *The Collegeville Pastoral Dictionary of Biblical Theology* (Collegeville, MN: The Liturgical Press, 1996), pp. 154-157.

Berne, E., *Beyond Games and Scripts* (New York: Grove Press, 1976).

Bingaman, K., "Christianity and the Shadow Side of Human Experience," *Pastoral Psychology* 49, no. 3 (January 2001), pp. 167-180.

Bradshaw, J., *Healing the Shame That Binds You* (Deerfield Beach: Health Communications, 1988).

Browning, D., *The Moral Context of Care* (Philadelphia: Westminster Press, 1976).

———, *Religious Ethics and Pastoral Care* (Minneapolis: Fortress Press, 1983).

———, *Religious Thought and the Modern Psychologies* (Philadephia: Fortress Press, 1987).

Browning, D. and Browning, C., "The Church and the Family Crisis: A New Love Ethic," *The Christian Century* 108, no. 23 (August 7, 1991), pp. 746-749.

Bruce, F.F., *Commentary on Galatians* (Exeter: The Paternoster Press, 1982).

Burns, D., *Feeling Good: The New Mood Therapy* (New York: Morrow, 1980).

Moving Toward Spiritual Maturity
© 2007 by The Haworth Press, Inc. All rights reserved.
doi:10.1300/5886_12

Burton-Christie, D., "Into the Body of Another: *Eros*, Embodiment and Intimacy with the Natural World," *Anglican Theological Review* 81, no. 1 (Winter 1999), pp. 13-37.

Callahan, W., *Noisy Contemplation* (Hyattsville, MD: Quixote Center, 1983).

Campbell, A., *Rediscovering Pastoral Care,* 2nd ed. (London: Darton, Longman and Todd, 1986).

Carr, A., *A Search for Wisdom and Spirit: Thomas Merton's Theology of Self* (Notre Dame, IN: University of Notre Dame Press, 1988).

Collins, T., "The Physiology of Tears in the Old Testament: Part I," *Catholic Biblical Quarterly* 33 (1971), pp. 18-38.

Dreyer, E., *Earth Crammed with Heaven* (New York: Paulist Press, 1994).

Erikson, E.H., *Identity: Youth and Crisis* (New York: W.W. Norton, 1968).

Fowler, J., *Becoming Adult, Becoming Christian* (Melbourne: Dove Communications, 1984).

Galbraith, D., *Music in the Listening Place.* Unpublished manuscript.

Grant, B., *The Social Structure of Christian Families* (St. Louis: Chalice Press, 2000).

Gula, R., *Reason Informed by Faith* (Mahwah, NJ: Paulist Press, 1989).

———, "Conscience," in B. Hoose, ed., *Christian Ethics: An Introduction* (London: Cassell, 1998), pp. 110-122.

Hall, C.S. and Nordby, V.J., *A Primer of Jungian Psychology* (New York: Mentor, 1973).

Hanson, P., *The People Called: The Growth of Community in the Bible* (San Francisco: Harper & Row, 1986).

Harris, T., *I'm Okay—You're Okay* (London: Jonathan Cape, 1973).

Hassel, D., *Radical Prayer* (New York: Paulist Press, 1983).

Hauerwas, S., *Character and the Christian Life: A Study in Theological Ethics* (San Antonio: Trinity University Press, 1975).

———, *Vision and Virtue* (Notre Dame, IN: University of Notre Dame Press, 1981).

Hitlin, S., "Values As the Core of Personal Identity: Drawing Links Between Two Theories of Self," *Social Psychology Quarterly* 66, no. 2 (June 2003), pp. 118-137.

Hoskins, M. and Loseho, J., "Changing Metaphors of the Self: Implications for Counseling," *Journal of Counseling and Development* 74, no. 3 (January-February 1996), pp. 243-252.

Howe, L., "The Family God Intends," *Journal of Pastoral Care* 53, no. 3 (Fall 1999), pp. 285-293.

Hutch, R., "Confessing Dying Within," *Journal of Pastoral Care* 48, no. 4 (Winter 1994), pp. 341-352.

Johnstone, B., "Solidarity and Moral Conscience: Challenges for Our Theological and Pastoral Work," *Studia Moralia* 31 (1993), pp. 65-85.

Jones, A., *Exploring Spiritual Direction* (Cambridge, MA: Cowley Publications, 1982, 1999).

Jones, S., "Rational-Emotive Therapy in Christian Perspective," *Journal of Psychology and Theology* 17 (Summer 1989), pp. 110-120.

Jung, C.G., *Psychological Reflections* (London: Routledge and Kegan Paul, 1971).

————, *Two Essays in Analytical Psychology,* 2nd ed. (Princeton, NJ: Princeton University Press, 1972).

————, *Aion,* 2nd ed., 5th printing (Princeton, NJ: Princeton University Press, 1978).

————, (ed.), *Man and His Symbols* (London: Picador, 1978). First published in 1964.

Karen, R., "Shame," *Atlantic Monthly* (February 1992), pp. 40-70.

Käsemann, E., *Commentary on Romans* (Grand Rapids: Eerdmans, 1980).

Kennedy, T., *Who Is Worthy?* (Sydney: Pluto Press, 2000).

Kohut, H., *The Restoration of the Self* (New York: International Universities Press, 1977).

————, "Remarks About the Formation of the Self: Letter to a Student Regarding Some Principles of Psychoanalytic Research," in P. Orstein, ed., *The Search for the Self,* vol. 2 (New York: International Universities Press, 1978), pp. 737-770.

Köster, H., *"Splánchnon,"* in G. Kittel and G. Friedrich, eds., *Theological Dictionary of the New Testament,* vol. 1, ed., trans., G. Bromiley (Grand Rapids: Eerdmans, 1985), pp. 1067-1069.

Leon-Dufour, X., "Mercy," in *Dictionary of Biblical Theology,* 2nd ed., updated, trans. P. Cahill and E. Stewart (London: Geoffrey Chapman, 1988), pp. 351-354.

Lewis, H.B., *Shame and Guilt in Neurosis* (New York: International Universities Press, 1971).

Little, G., *Strong Leadership* (Melbourne: Oxford University Press, 1988).

Mair, J.M.M., "The Community of Self," in D. Bannister, ed., *New Perspectives in Personal Construct Theory* (London: Academic Press, 1977), pp. 125-149.

Malone, T., "Self-Fulfillment Through Service to Others," *The Humanist* 49, no. 1 (January 1989), p. 49.

Marcel, G. "Phenomenological Notes on Being in a Situation," in his *Creative Fidelity* (New York: The Noonday Press, 1964).

Markus, H. and Nurius, P., "Possible Selves," *American Psychologist* 41, no. 9 (September 1986), pp. 954-969.

Maslow, A., *The Farther Reaches of Human Nature* (Harmondsworth: Penguin Books, 1973).

May, R., *Love and Will* (New York: W.W. Norton, 1969).

————, *Man's Search for Himself* (London: Souvenir Press, 1975).

Mayer, S., "High-Risk Perfectionism," *Human Development* 20, no. 1 (Spring 1999), pp. 5-8.

Merton, T., *Seeds of Contemplation* (London: Burns and Oates, 1949, 1957).

————, *The New Man* (New York: Farrar, Straus and Giroux, 1961, 2000).

————, *Contemplative Prayer* (New York: Image Books, 1971, 1996).

————, *Conjectures of a Guilty Bystander* (Garden City, New York: Double Day, Image Books, 1968).

————, *Contemplation in a World of Action* (Notre Dame, IN: University of Notre Dame Press, 1998, 2003).

Miller-McLemore, B.J., *Also a Mother* (Nashville: Abingdon Press, 1994).

Moore, T., "Spiritualities of Depth," *Tikkun* 13, no. 6 (November/December 1998), pp. 40-41.

Morris, L., *The Epistle to the Romans* (Grand Rapids: Eerdmans, 1988).

Nangle, J., "A Spirituality of Ecology," *Sojourners* 27, no. 5 (September/October 1998), p. 54.

Nouwen, H., *The Wounded Healer* (Garden City, NY: Doubleday, 1972).

———, *Reaching Out* (Garden City, NY: Doubleday, 1975).

Nouwen, H., McNeill, D., and Morrison, D., *Compassion* (London: Darton, Longman and Todd, 1982).

Nygren, A., *Agape and Eros: Part I* (London: SPCK, 1932).

———, *Agape and Eros: Part II* (London: SPCK, 1939).

Outka, G., *Agape: An Ethical Analysis* (New Haven: Yale University Press, 1972).

———, "Universal Love and Impartiality," in E. Santuri and W. Werpehowski, eds., *The Love Commandments: Essays in Christian Ethics and Moral Philosophy* (Washington: Georgetown University Press, 1992), pp. 1-103.

Overman, J.A., *Church and Community in Crisis: The Gospel According to Matthew* (Valley Forge, PA: Trinity Press International, 1996).

Pattison, S., *Shame: Theory, Therapy, Theology* (New York: Cambridge University Press, 2000).

Pazola, R., "Sacred: What Native Americans Believe," *U.S. Catholic* 59, no. 2 (February 1994), pp. 16-23.

Pembroke, N., *The Art of Listening* (Grand Rapids: Eerdmans, 2002).

Percy, W., *The Second Coming* (New York: Farrar, Straus and Giroux, 1980).

Peterson, E., *Working the Angles* (Grand Rapids: Eerdmans, 1987).

Plantinga, C., *Not the Way It's Supposed to Be: A Breviary of Sin* (Grand Rapids: Eerdmans,1995).

Porter, J., *The Recovery of Virtue: The Relevance of Aquinas for Christian Ethics* (Louisville: Westminster/John Knox Press, 1990).

Post, S., "Communion and True Self-Love," *Journal of Religious Ethics* 16 (Fall 1988), pp. 345-362.

———, "The Inadequacy of Selflessness," *Journal of the American Academy of Religion* 56, no. 2 (1989), pp. 213-228.

Roberts, R.C., "The Troubled Self—Me, Myself, & I: How Far Should We Go in Our Search for Self-Fulfillment?" *Christianity Today* 37, no. 7 (June 21, 1993), p. 37.

Rowan, J., *Subpersonalities: The People Inside Us* (London: Routledge, 1990).

Rowe, D., *Wanting Everything: The Art of Happiness* (London: Fontana, 1991).

Rubio, J.H., *A Christian Theology of Marriage and Family* (New York: Paulist Press, 2003).

Sperry, L., *Transforming Self and Community: Revisioning Pastoral Counseling and Spiritual Direction* (Collegeville: Liturgical Press, 2002).

Stone, B., *Compassionate Ministry* (Maryknoll: Orbis Books, 1996).

Stone, H. and Winkelman, S., *Embracing Our Selves* (Marina del Rey, CA: Devorss and Co., 1985).

Vacek, E., *Love, Human and Divine: The Heart of Christian Ethics* (Washington, DC: Georgetown University Press, 1994).

von Franz, M-L., "The Process of Individuation," in C. Jung, ed., *Man and His Symbols* (London: Picador, 1978). First published in 1964.

Index